WHAT'S WRONG WITH ME?

Dr. LINDA L. MOORE

BY THE AUTHOR

Release from Powerlessness: Take Charge of Your Life

Cover design by Liz Newell

ISBN-13: 978-1492254874
ISBN-10: 1492254878

DEDICATION

For the hundreds and hundreds of women who have touched my life and impacted my thinking – clients, workshop participants colleagues and friends. Thank you

TABLE OF CONTENTS

Acknowledgments — i

Introduction — ii

How to Use this Book — iii

1 Question One: What's Wrong With Me? Why Do I Feel So Crazy? — 1

2 Question Two: Why Can't I Cope With My Problems By Myself? — 27

3 Question Three: What If People Knew What I _Really_ Think and Feel? — 40

4 Question Four: What If I Lose Control – Start to Cry or Get Angry and Can't Stop? — 55

5 Question Five: What If I Look Inside And There Is Nothing There Or I Hate What I Find? — 73

6 Question Six: Why Do I Feel Like Such A Chile? So Incompetent? — 85

7 Question Seven: Why Can't I Have A Good Relationship? Why Do I Keep Failing? — 98

8 Question Eight: Why Can't I Count On Anyone? — 114

9 Question Nine: What If I'm Like My Mother? — 138

10 Question Ten: Why Do I Do Such Terrible, Self-Destructive Things To Myself? — 160

11 Question Eleven: What's Wrong With Men? — 174

12 Question Twelve: Are You Ready To Take Your Power Back? — 192

13 Question Thirteen: How Can I Get Started? Your Checklists For Power, Change and Self Care? — 216

Appendix A — 226

Appendix B — 234

Appendix C — 236

Contact Information — 238

About The Author — 239

ACKNOWLEDGEMENTS

Although writing a book often feels like a solitary journey, in reality it's the opposite. It's not possible to enter and finally exit the process without many others. Thanks to Liz Newell – the tech expert who puts "everything" together! To Jo-Lynne Worley and Joanie Shoemaker for reading early versions and providing excellent feedback. Much gratitude to Deborah Shouse for masterful editing skills – and to dear friends Kay Barnes, Laura Shultz and Merle Moores for support and nudging – and to Rick and Jeanie Moore – solid anchors in my life.

INTRODUCTION

Listening to so many women for so many years has convinced me that we are always questioning ourselves and our lives. My focus in this book is on the *universality* and the *negativity* of the questions women ask. One basic thread connects the underlying content of the questions, as well as the feelings and beliefs that produce them – the absence of power – the inability to be the person who is in charge of her own life.

In *Release from Powerlessness: Take Charge of Your Life*, I asked two healthy questions about power when making presentations to women's groups. The answers were so often negative, I was motivated to explore how the "absence of power" distorts thinking – creating the questions that cause most women to feel stuck and defeated vs motivated to change!

I've identified eleven questions that appear to be common, if not universal, among women. Each is negative and self-defeating. If you ask it yourself, you probably do so when you feel "powerless."

The questions come from the combined voices of many women – clients and seminar participants, voices of dear friends, colleagues and associates – and of course mine. Women from all walks of life, professions, and from the most varied life experiences ask these questions.

I explore the reasons for asking such negative questions; share clients' negative answers; teach the process of "reframing" the questions; and provide *new* questions that lead to growth, change, happiness and power.

Use this workbook and these questions to learn to re-frame your thinking – alter and re-charge your *brain* in a healthy and positive direction, and step into the life space you desire.

If and when you see yourself in these pages, may it be with empathy, perhaps a touch of humor and the insight for change.

HOW TO USE THIS BOOK

There are several ways to use this book. Here are my suggestions.

-Read through the entire book to understand the questions, the theory, and the useful tool of writing without answering the questions. Then return to chapter one and answer the questions.

-Write in the body of the book as you read or turn to blank pages provided in the appendix or use a separate notebook.

-Turn to a chapter that has a question that really speaks to you and your current challenges and start there.

-Whatever you choose to do, please take the time to write your thoughts and feelings. It really helps make change more possible.

-When it feels like hard work or just too stressful, see if you can continue for 5 or 10 more minutes. If it's still too hard, take a break.

-If at any time you feel over whelmed or just far too stressed, talk to a friend, a family member or consider asking for help from a therapist, physician, or minister. You can also open my website and email your questions directly to me. I will help however I can. Your self care, your ability to create healthy change is the goal..

CHAPTER ONE

QUESTION ONE: "WHAT'S WRONG WITH ME? WHY DO I FEEL SO CRAZY?

An intense and inflammatory question! And the best answer is "nothing *but* the question." Reality? There is a high degree of probability that absolutely nothing is wrong with you and you are definitely not crazy. However, you may be asking negative and self defeating questions often enough to convince yourself that there *is* something wrong – to have your mind traveling so often in the wrong direction for self exploration you create self doubt, bump into insurmountable walls in your thinking and feeling, and end up depressed or anxious – or both.

Take a minute and examine the question: How often do you hear yourself ask: What's wrong with me? Several times a week? Several times a day? If you acknowledge the question is in your head, you are probably feeling a great deal of stress – unnecessary and undeserved stress, anxiety and depression. You truly can feel better!

HOW COMMON ARE THESE NEGATIVE QUESTIONS? ARE YOU SURE IT'S NOT JUST ME?

I regularly hear what's wrong with me? Do you think I'm crazy? And the other negative questions throughout the boo – from clients, seminar and workshop participants, and friends.

A FRIEND AND BUSINESS ASSOCIATE

At lunch with my friend, Helen, she leaned across the table and said, "Please tell me what's wrong with me!" And it was certainly not the first time I'd heard this from her.

"Can I get you to stop asking that?" I said. It was frustrating for me because Helen has a truly successful life!

I've known Helen for many years, and periodically she falls into a deep hole of self doubt. She questions herself for days and then invites me to have lunch so she can ask me what I think is wrong with her. Actually, when you know her history, thinking so negatively is logical. She grew up with a mother and father who demanded perfection. Regardless of her accomplishments, she doubted her performance because her parents did not affirm her. No "good work" affirmations from either of them. Just high expectations. She came out of that upbringing never knowing "what is enough." Or "when have I done enough?" Or "am I good enough."

With a law degree and a PhD in economics, Helen still pushed herself to do more. Two relatively good marriages ended because she struggled with being able to define true happiness, or to accurately measure her own success as a partner. She questioned her parenting, even though her two grown children were successful and quite happy. She had been smart enough to "correct" the deficient parenting she received and alter her behavior with her kids.

The correction she failed to make was with herself. She continued to treat herself, judge herself, the way her parents treated and judged her.

Even though I had tried to be a helpful friend over the years, I realized I had to shift gears and encourage Helen to seriously examine how to take better care of herself beyond periodic lunch conversations. I told her about the draft of this book and asked if she would experiment and use the first few chapters to examine her negative thinking. She was comforted to hear that many, many women ask the question, and eagerly agreed.

A UNIVERSAL QUESTION

"What's wrong with me?" is a universal and disturbing female question. But there are reasons that help understand what causes many women, and perhaps you, to see themselves as defective.

From the many years I've worked with women and listened to the stories of our lives, I offer this basic observation: It is close to impossible to grow up female in our patriarchal culture and not ask yourself if you are okay, if you're doing it right, if there is something wrong with your perception or with you.

BUT I'M A NCE GIRL!…HOW DID THIS HAPPEN?

You learned, first as a little girl, then as a woman, that creating good relationships is your "job." More specifically it is a primary role "assignment" for women and girls. For generations of women, most of the problems in life have been about your effectiveness or ineffectiveness in those relationships – whether at home, at work, or in any other setting.

If it's your "job," it is logical that you see yourself as the source of the problem when something goes wrong.

BECAUSE……..

As women, you receive signals from all areas of your environment, from birth to

old age, that something about you is not quite "right."

- -You don't fit in here.

- -That is not the way we do things here.

- -You think differently, not as clearly and logically as men (and some women).

- -You display too many feelings.

- -You are too sensitive.

- -Your ideas are "just like a woman."

- -You're not practical.

- -You worry too much about relationships.

- -You just don't seem to "get it."

With these or similar statements and innuendos that grow into "beliefs," what would keep you from questioning yourself? What have you been taught to help you focus your doubts, at least first, anywhere but on yourself?

WHEN HAVE YOU FELT THE SAME THING?

Helen's questions about herself are typical of women. That fleeting thought that there is something seriously wrong with you – that perhaps you have finally "lost it" – comes when you tell yourself almost nothing is going right and your life is out of control. Even if a friend can point to all the things going well – as in Helen's "reality"—the thoughts are there.

>The questions, are triggered on those difficult days when:

>-You can't believe one more thing has gone wrong.

>-You're amazed by your ability to survive long enough to drag yourself into bed at the end of the day.

>-You are relieved just to have ended a difficult conversation alive.

>-You are so genuinely overwhelmed that you have no idea how to make it better.

The questions, asked often enough, turn into beliefs. Then you simply assume there is something wrong with you. The assumptions distort your perception of yourself and the life you are struggling to make better.

DON'T MEN ASK THE SAME QUESTIONS?

No. Women question themselves. Men question women.

Women ask:

>-"What's wrong with me?"

>-"What have I done wrong this time?"

Most women have been taught to look at themselves as the source of the difficulty. You quickly look inside – for the fault or the defect. Even when you attempt to focus on someone else, the doubt is running around in your head.

Men ask:

- "What's wrong with *you* ?"

The majority of men question you, someone else, or the situation, before they question themselves. Just as women have been taught to look inside, men have been taught to look outside; the self is not the first target for analysis.

LORNA'S CHALLENGE AT WORK

Lorna, a successful business woman, entered therapy because her interactions with some of her male colleagues puzzled and stressed her. She frequently came away from meetings, and even casual conversations feeling frustrated, angry and disappointed in her behavior. She was smart enough to know she was falling into some kind of emotional trap in her head, but she was still concerned "something was wrong."

Her most recent example was a conversation with a male peer about a hiring decision they needed to make together

She said: I think the third candidate we interviewed for the new position is our best choice. What about you?

He said: We do need to jump on this quickly. What do you like about her?

She said: Smart, experienced, energetic, a dynamic presence. And she is clearly qualified.

He said: Well, I'm not sure I agree with all that.

She said: You don't? (Lorna reported that *right* in that moment, she knew her comfort level had shifted and she had to push herself to stay focused).

He said: I'm just saying I'm not sure.

She said: Well, what do you think? (It was the right question but she knew she sounded frustrated and impatient. She just could not "calm" herself.)

He said: Shrugging, he repeated, "I'm *thinking* about it…." (now his tone became impatient; he avoided eye contact, frowned, looked at his watch)

She said: So think! (again she heard herself but failed to correct or modulate her tone).

He said: What's wrong with you today? (more frowns, critical looks, shrugged his shoulders, looked at his watch again)

She said: What do you mean? Why should there be something wrong?

He said: You just seem angry….

By now, Lorna had lost her train of thought entirely and intuitively knew the conversation was far off track. She felt defensive and unsure and was already busily examining "what *was* wrong with her?" Her self doubt truly ramped up the moment her colleague took himself off the hook to deal with the issue between them (a male behavior that is common, even if unconscious) with "what's wrong with you today?" And "you just seem angry." Whatever his motivation – and it could have honestly just been he had not made up his mind, didn't really know which candidate he preferred and did not wish to be pushed into a decision—he redirected the conversation away from his own indecision to Lorna's "mood." And she allowed that to happen.

They ended the conversation unsuccessfully, and she returned to her office to try to sort out what had happened. She truly knew what she wanted to say and do but was totally confused about what got in her way.

Lorna began this conversation professionally and appropriately. And if she could have stayed with the content of the conversation, she might have accomplished her objective; however, she was triggered by her colleague's nonverbal behavior, voice tone, the lack of clarity of his thoughts, and finally by the question he asked her about "being okay."

At that point, her own negative thoughts and feelings high jacked her brain.

"Staying connected" is a strong motivator for most women. That includes a need for agreement, lack of conflict and elimination of differences. It can also extend to a need for approval, affirmation, and sometimes a need for a similar approach to a problem regardless of the content. In other words if you "think what I think, feel what I feel, and do it the way I do it" things will be okay!

And what happened to the original agenda? Lost. Lorna lost focus on the intent to hire a new employee. She was thinking about her ineffective communication, her defensiveness, her failure to accomplish the goal for the meeting.

How often do you get off track in any of your conversations – with men or with other women? Failing to accomplish your primary agenda as Lorna did happens most often when:

-the other person, especially if it's an important relationship, gets you to focus on what's wrong with you rather than the topic of conversation.

-you have a need to be right, to have the other person agree with your thoughts and feelings and ideas of what to do.

WHO IS RIGHT? WHO IS WRONG? WHAT'S THE RIGHT ANSWER?

Again, it's the wrong question. This is about failed communication and the contribution each person made to the breakdown of the original agenda. In an ideal world, women learn to question the man, the other person, and the situation, as well as themselves. Men learn to question themselves as well as questioning you, others and the situation. The ability to look both inside and outside creates a healthy individual who comes to a conversation centered and powerful and able to negotiate beyond differences, manage conflict, and make the best decision possible.

THE SHORT END OF THE STICK

While waiting for the ideal world to get here, or more proactively planning for it, women end up on the short end of the stick. In conversations where women question only themselves, they lose. The man gets the "upper hand" emotionally and dominates the content and focus. The woman ends up feeling bad about herself and loses focus on her legitimate agenda.

SO WHY FOCUS ON WOMEN?

Women have been taught to question themselves – negatively and unproductively. You can identify the negative questions you ask yourself, and then learn to stop doing it. You can learn to look outside yourself for the source of the problem – when appropriate. That balanced analysis of the "self and the system" can put you on a more level playing field with the men you live with or work with, like and love. And the analysis can obviously help you with your relationships with other women.

A REMINDER

When you continue to examine yourself to find what's wrong with you, remember this: "Sometimes the reason you feel crazy is because you are in a crazy situation. Not feeling crazy may be the thing that means you really are. That makes feeling crazy the only possible sane response!"

Translation: Trust your intuitive sense of the environment – the situation – the event, as well as who you are and what you feel. Examine the external as well as the internal. Generally women are too quick to look inside for the source of the difficulty and to stop right there. Always study what's going on around you, making sure you understand your environment. The questions we've learned to ask ourselves keep us stuck in self-examination, avoiding the necessary analysis of external circumstances crucial to total understanding.

ASSUMPTIONS MADE MARILYN FEEL CRAZY!

> Marilyn had been in therapy with me for about one month but she wasn't really communicating with me. She held back, behaved in a reticent, even slightly frightened manner. I had laid the groundwork for her to feel safe, but something was missing. She told me the surface facts about her life, and carefully avoided talking about her feelings.

> "My life is going just perfectly," Marilyn typically explained, always smiling, her expression strained. Then at the end of an appointment, she clenched her hands, burst into tears, and exclaimed. "So why is my hair

falling out and why do I feel so terrible?"

Marilyn was in an extremely complex situation, yet she appeared to be completely "in control." She was in a third marriage with six children. Three were hers from previous marriages, two were her husband's, and one was the child of her current marriage. She was in a new executive position, and very pleased at having recently been promoted. On the down side, she had been asked to take over a problem-ridden department and make it work. She and her husband were completing the last steps in building a new home. "I am happy with my life," she insisted. "But, I'm jumpy and irritable. I can't sleep, I'm losing weight. And I'm angry with everyone – Jim, the kids, my employees. I'm surprised anyone wants to be around me."

A complete physical exam had revealed nothing. But her symptoms were real and serious. Her life appeared ideal by all the external measures, and yet she was losing her hair!

A SHIFT TAKES PLACE

"Marilyn, most women in your situation would be convinced they were going crazy," I said. "I am worried about your symptoms, and I know we have to work hard together to figure out what's going on, but I want you to know I don't think you are crazy."

She looked somewhat startled. A few tears leaked out around the corners of her eyes. A minute passed before she said, "I've been terrified I'm losing my mind! How could I be like this when my life is going so well? Do you really think there's nothing terribly wrong with me?"

I affirmed my belief in her sanity, and we began to work at a deeper, more honest level. Once her fears were out in the open, Marilyn released months of pent up feelings, examined the specifics that were causing so much stress. She was over extended and looking at what *she* needed to do differently rather than delegating, including her executives in hard decisions, or examining ways she could change the system. We looked at the changes she needed to make. In a few months she was doing great, living a complex but rich life – and with all her hair!

Giving up the conclusion that there was something wrong with her wasn't easy. She was gradually able to see the benefits of a balanced analysis of herself and of "the system" – her relationships, her family, her department, her organization, even society's expectations of her as a woman. Her ability to look at all these aspects of her life, and ask healthy questions, diminished the constant self-doubt and led to the decisions that put her back in charge.

THE "LOGIC" OF SELF-BLAME

When you are truly confused about what's wrong, and don't have much permission to express your feelings, (someone might think they are inappropriate or quite unacceptable), self-blame can seem logical. When you are uncomfortable with your anger or feel inadequate in a conflict, self-blame is seductive. If you're the problem, maybe you can actually do something about it.

Blaming yourself can mask a much larger problem in a relationship, a job, or a long-standing conflict. If you're the problem, you avoid looking at other people or situations that will demand some major changes. That way you don't have to be angry and you don't have to face an uncomfortable conflict.

A PERSONAL DISCOVERY ABOUT SELF-DOUBT AND BLAME

Several years ago I was speaking to an audience of about 2000 women about self-esteem. I was holding the microphone and making the point about the destructiveness of self-blame, when I suddenly became aware that my voice had stopped carrying over the sound system. I immediately looked to see if I had turned the mic off. I did not think, "The system has failed." I automatically assumed that I had done something wrong and had messed up the system. I was the problem. The feeling surged out of the old tapes in my head.

The sound system was quickly attended to, and I shared my thoughts with the audience. As I did, a giant wave of laughter spread among the women. It was the laughter of shared relief – of knowing that almost every woman in that room understood what I had felt because they had felt something similar so often – if so many of us have felt it, we couldn't all really be the problem – at least not all the time!

ASKING THE WRONG QUESTIONS!

If you think it's always your fault, you're in good company. Almost all little girls and women conclude they are the source of the problem and question what's wrong!

Questioning yourself isn't wrong. It's the questions themselves that are wrong. When they are negative and self-defeating, your mind generates answers that create more negative feelings, more discouraging thoughts, and the hole you are in gets deeper and darker. You paralyze yourself – get stuck – with thoughts like these.

"I just can't seem to do it right. Why do I always do it wrong?"

"I'm tired of feeling this way. I can't change. I'm sick and tired of being the one who's wrong. Why can't I ever do anything right?"

"I keep wondering if I'm just stressed, but I know I have to figure out what's wrong with me?

"I'm always the problem. Why can't I get it right just once?"

"I'm afraid I'm finally losing it. I just cry so easily. What if I can't stop?"

"Nothing I do goes right. What if I just can't fix it?"

These questions and assumptions are destructive to self-esteem and lead you away from identifying the problem and solving it. Then you think you are the problem, and that your thoughts or your feelings are "crazy."

NO MORE CONDITIONED QUESTIONING

If you are not the problem, what are you? Conditioned! Conditioned to ask, "What's wrong with me?" Conditioned to believe you are the problem. Even when the question you ask is about someone else and what's wrong with them, you may be struggling with doubt about yourself. You can change that.

Give up seeing yourself as the source of the problem and learn to see yourself as the source of the solution. That shift means realizing you are the only person who can take responsibility for making your life better. A first step is to start asking healthy questions in order to start problem-solving, to change.

GETTING STARTED WITH QUESTIONS THAT WORK

It is essential to ask healthy questions, and equally important to recognize a question that is heading you in the wrong direction. You can "reframe" questions so that you tap into the smart, healthy part of you that wants to change.

EVALUATING AND REFRAMING QUESTIONS

Any question you ask yourself more than once needs to be "checked out," but those particularly dangerous to your mental health are the ones you ask all the time – like "What's wrong with me? Why do I feel so crazy?"

When turning a question into one that works, keep these principles in mind:

-A question with *why* in it automatically makes your mind go in the wrong direction. Change it to what, when, where, or how. Instead of "<u>Why</u> am I doing this?" Ask, "<u>What</u> am I doing?"

-When questions include other people, describe their actions and behaviors.

"Why does he do these terrible things to me?" gets you no where fast. There is no answer that will satisfy you! Substitute "<u>What</u> (behavior) does he engage in that is so hard for me?"

-Eliminate generalizations like "always," "never," "every time." These are the words that make an already difficult situation feel worse. They imply nothing is ever the way you want it: "Every time I talk to her we have a fight." Maybe "much of the time" or "frequently" is more realistic. It's important to be accurate to get your brain working better!

-Avoid emotionally loaded words. "Crazy" is a perfect example because it has dozens of negative connotations and images attached to it. If you describe yourself as crazy, your mind goes in the worst possible direction. You begin to feel you can't be fixed! Search for a word that fits: angry, lonely, frightened, sad, overwhelmed.

-Other examples of emotionally loaded words are "terrible or awful." Identify substitute words or phrases that are descriptive of behavior or specific feelings. Instead of "Why do I get myself into terrible relationships and feel so awful, so crazy?" try "What is making me feel so sad or frightened?"

-Either/or words also need to be eliminated. "Good/bad or right/wrong limit your thinking. "What is wrong with me? Am I just a bad person?" is the most dramatic example. It implies and assumes a personal defect that you must find – and fix. "What is going on in my life that is creating sadness or pain?" is much more specific. It makes you search for behavior and specific situations rather than character defects – like craziness.

Evaluated and reframed, the original questions, "What is wrong with me? Why do I feel so crazy?" become: "What is happening in my life that creates so much confusion and unhappiness? What is going on that causes me to feel such intense pain?" Or "What is going on that feels so negative? What is happening when I label my feelings crazy?" Take a minute for reflection and write your own version.

TESTING THE DIFFERENCE

The new questions may not seem all that different to you, so try an experiment. Ask yourself the original question again – "What's wrong with me? Why do I feel so crazy?" and write down every thought that comes to you. Try writing quickly without reflecting or editing. You are the only person who will read this.

-Check to see what you are feeling as you write. You might discover you are angry, even a little "worked up." Perhaps you feel sad or lonely, defeated or overwhelmed. Make notes:

-What are you thinking? Are the thoughts discouraging? The same ones you have been having for some time? Again, make notes:

-What do you feel physically? Is your stomach or chest tight? Do you feel hot or flushed? Is your jaw clenched? Your shoulders and ear lobes starting to touch? Or do you find your body sagging? Write anything you are aware of:

WHAT DO MY ANSWERS MEAN?

There are no right or wrong responses. You simply want to see what you are thinking, feeling, experiencing physically. Write or reflect on what you observe.

RELAX A MINUTE, THEN EXPERIMENT.

Take a deep breath, relax. Imagine eliminating that question from your mind, erasing it with a giant eraser. Ask yourself the new, reframed question: "What are the circumstances in my life and what is happening that creates so much confusion and unhappiness?" "What is happening in my life when I label my feelings crazy?" Use this example or write your own.

-Write anything that comes into your mind. Write quickly and don't edit.

-Check your feelings.

-Check your thoughts.

-Check your physical sensations.

Compare your answers to both questions. What are the differences in your answers? In your feelings? In your thoughts? In your body? Look for even a subtle shift. Make a note of anything you are conscious of, even if it is no change at all.

WHAT SHOULD HAPPEN WHEN I REFRAME A QUESTION?

There are no "shoulds," but if you keep trying the techniques as you continue to read, you will notice that you feel better when you reframe the negative questions you ask. The most important outcome is a better definition of the problems you are facing; an understanding of what you really think and feel; and consequently, a clearer idea of what and how to change.

WHAT MAKES CHANGE SO HARD?

Change hurts. Change is a form of loss. We grieve change. Consequently, you might be resisting it. You may be beating up on yourself, blaming others, or finding millions of ways to avoid doing what you may know – at this minute, in the wisest part of your being – you need to do. Women often blind themselves to the environment – what they see and know needs to change – and continue to look inside with a critical, doubting eye. When you learn to look both outside and inside in a positive, non-blaming manner, you discover options you couldn't have imagined before.

BUT, PERSONALLY, I RESIST CHANGE

Historically, my first response to a proposed change was often an automatic reflex: "No!" I am embarrassed to say that reaction sometimes easily pops into my head around even small or seemingly insignificant things. For example: A good friend who is an interior designer and I were sitting in my living room discussing some artwork I wanted to hang. She suggested: "Let's try moving this piece into the hallway."

"No, I don't want to move that!" I blurted out. I heard my tone, and saw the astonished look on her face. I was clearly upset with her for suggesting a change. Quite surprised by my intense, inappropriate response, I took a few deep breaths, and reflected on what I was feeling.

In that moment, I was irrationally uncomfortable, even a little frightened – I felt, and acted, like a little girl who was wrong, and consequently, in trouble. I wanted to be right and in control. Because I'm familiar with such momentary regressive feelings, I could see the situation as a signal to focus what I know about myself and talk about it.

I told my friend what I was feeling – resistance to change, a flash of fear of being out of control, followed by anger. I also shared I sometimes have to push myself to try new ways of doing things. Then I suggested we try her changes, extracting a promise it was only an experiment. Her idea was excellent. I was able to laugh at myself and do it her way. It was such a small request for change, I knew it had triggered something *else* in me. Later that day, I reflected and re-examined old experiences that contributed to my difficulty with change.

PROBLEMS WITH CHANGE START IN CHILDHOOD

As a child I frequently came home from school to find all the furniture rearranged. My mother cleaned, painted, wallpapered, and moved furniture obsessively! I didn't like it when she quite frequently changed my bedroom without telling me. I felt I had to accept it, but decided: "When I have my own house, I will keep things right where I want them." I didn't know I had made that powerful childhood decision until through the years, I observed I sometimes felt conflict and over-reacted to changes in my life. And in this situation, about the simple task of hanging a painting! Historically, conflicts, even arguments about "big" changes didn't always motivate me to question my resistance. It seemed legitimate. Seeing the intensity of my reaction, especially around a truly simple decision, helped me understand more about my resistance to change and my preference that "others" do the changing instead of me.

I can't suggest that change is easy, but I know there is no one I've yet encountered who couldn't improve themselves by facing the needed changes in their lives. The happiest people appear to be those who finally understand this and decide to do something about it.

IT TAKES PSYCHOLOGICAL MUSCLE

Changing means you are ready to get realistic with yourself about what's really happening in your life. Ask yourself some healthy questions. Start with the ones at the end of this chapter. Use the workbook section, in addition to the space provided in each chapter, to answer questions and identify the things you would like to do differently. If you discover your list is long, that means hard work. Consequently, it is essential to do one thing at a time.

Each small success helps you develop "psychological muscle." Think of that bulge in your bicep, no matter how small, as a metaphor for your "change muscle." It has to be developed and maintained. It necessitates your consistent attention, regardless of the temporary pain.

A VISUAL IMAGE FOR CHANGE

As you start your change process, visualize old familiar behavior as a deep, wide groove in your brain. It's dark, somewhat cozy in its familiarity regardless of how bad it may be for you. See the behavior you want to switch to as a tiny little dent in your brain. It's bright and fresh, but unfamiliar and scary, regardless of how good it is for you. When you are centered, and in charge you can more readily decide to behave in a new way. When you are stressed, exhausted, angry, or shamed, you will pick the familiar behavior.

That deep groove is recognizable! Early in the change process, the new, tiny dent can hardly be seen or remembered. Consequently, while you are still learning new behavior, you will naturally slip, back-slide, and fail to do it the way you want.

When you experience failure, analyze it. See what you can learn. What triggers set you off in the wrong direction? Who were you talking to? Where were you? What were you thinking and feeling? Use your mistakes. And keep practicing the new behavior.

RESULTS! SUCCESS!

Each time you have a success at least two things happen. Your "psychological muscle" gets bigger and stronger; and that tiny dent in your brain deepens. It begins to form a groove. Eventually, when the new groove is as deep as the old one, real choice is less of a struggle. The new behavior has become familiar. It feels good. It is good for you. You know it throughout your system. You're changing. You are making your life better. You really can do it!

A NEW APPROACH

Remember: It's not always you! What is the other person doing? What is the family, the organization, or the larger system you are dealing with like? In raising these questions, keep your eye on the fine line between looking at "the other" in order to describe or understand it, rather than to blame it and insist it change.

A LIGHT BULB FOR ANNIE, A REMINDER FOR YOU!

If you really do have trouble either believing or sustaining the belief that you might not be the problem, that it's not always your fault, keep this saying from the beginning of the chapter in mind:

"Sometimes the reason you feel crazy is because you are in a crazy situation. Not feeling crazy may be the thing that means you really are. And that makes feeling crazy the only possible sane response."

I usually have to repeat that twice in workshops and presentations. Spontaneous laughter is the general response. But the best reaction came from Annie, a college administrator, who said: "You mean that if I picked a 100% certified, healthy, competent woman and put her in my job, she would be just as stressed as I am in six months? And that could be because I am working in a truly crazy-making environment?"

I nodded, and indicated, "It's certainly possible. It will help if you examine your work environment in detail. Look for the specific events or interactions that create those overwhelmed feelings before passing judgment on yourself."

She sighed with relief, stating, "Then maybe I'm not the problem after all – at least not the total problem. I think I've known that for a long time, but I've had trouble trusting my perception."

ENDING THE RUSH TO JUDGMENT

If you believe there is something wrong with you and once in a while you feel a little crazy, you need some relief. Start by questioning your question. If it's all about how terrible you are, it's the wrong one. If it has no inquiry about the situations you find yourself in, it's the wrong one.

IS THERE A GOOD ANSWER TO THE NEGATIVE QUESTION?

If you continue to have trouble eliminating the negative question – "What's wrong with me? Why do I feel so crazy?" – try answering it with a definitive *NO!*

"No, I am not crazy. I am facing some painful, frightening feelings and some difficult situations. I need to be patient with myself as I work to figure out what to do – how to take care of myself.

A BASIC ANALYSIS: THE BEGINNING OF CHANGE

When you're ready, answer the questions below. That can be right now, or when you've completed the book, or when something else moves you to take some time to sit down, reflect, and hopefully, write. If you write now, your answers can serve as a good basis for reading and reflecting in the chapters to come. If you do it later, you will approach the questions with a new perspective. Choose what works for you. Keep what you write so you can re-examine your thoughts and feelings. You may discover you have things to add, change, or reconsider as you learn more about yourself, about all the negative questions in your head, and most important, how you can change them.

-What is happening in your life that you don't like?

-What are the things/who are the people you don't feel good about?

-What feelings or behaviors do you have that you have labeled as "just a little crazy?"

-What changes are needed to make your life better?

-When you think of making changes, what do you feel?

-What did you learn about change growing up? Were you encouraged? Discouraged? Pressured? Ignored?

-What kind of change did you observe growing up? For example, did you see someone successfully stop drinking or smoking? Accomplish a desired goal? Did you witness frequent failure?

-What have you observed about change throughout your life? If it helps, break your lists/writing into blocks of time: ages 1-7; 7-14; 14-21; etc.

-List the things you have tried to change but believe you have failed.

-Examine your list. Look for relationships, patterns. What have you learned from your failures? If all your answers are negative, push yourself to identify any positives.

-What are the things you don't know how to handle? The problems you need help solving?

-What resources are available to you? Your own skills, abilities, attitudes? Who are the people/what are the places for the information you need?

Finally.......

This is a process of examining what you think and how that impacts your decisions and consequent behavior. If it feels daunting, just read the entire book, and then return to the challenge of answering the questions. You can do it!

CHAPTER TWO

QUESTION TWO: "WHY CAN'T I COPE WITH MY PROBLEMS BY MYSELF?

Be right! Be good! Be Perfect! Look like you are doing fine even when you feel terrible. The pressure to be responsible begins, for many, the moment you're wrapped in the pink blanket. Women are expected to be the "emotional caretakers of the world" – with a smile on their faces.

DID ANYONE EVER TELL YOU TO PUT YOURSELF FIRST?

Since you're expected to care for others, you feel a failure when you need to ask for help. When you do finally request assistance for yourself, you may feel self-conscious and remorseful. If your financial situation is tight or stretched, the bad feelings about paying someone for assistance are even greater. What if someone else in the family needed money more than you! Besides, wouldn't it be better if you just figured this out by yourself?

Years ago I saw a television commercial portraying an adult daughter and her mother arguing in the kitchen about cooking. Finally, the exasperated daughter, waved a skillet in her hand and said: "I'd rather do it myself!"

The unspoken message, represented multiple layers of feelings. "I want to do it myself." "I should be able to do it myself." And, finally, "I don't want anyone (especially my mother) to know that I can't do it myself." She, after all, is likely to be the person who taught you to be so overly self-sufficient in the first place!

BUT I THINK I'M A FAILURE!

"Why can't I cope with my problems by myself?" Many women, unconsciously, keep themselves from getting information, instruction, therapy, even medical attention by continuing to ask the question over and over. Many women continue to labor with "Why can't I do this myself," even when they are in therapy .

Some women have made this same negative inquiry while on the phone exploring making a first appointment. The topic also comes up frequently in your conversations when you discuss your "lack of ability to manage your lives." It creeps into the unspoken thoughts of most women. And it has attached questions: "How come I need therapy when no one else does?" And, "What is wrong with me, anyway?" is always lurking underneath the surface!

LISTEN TO THE THOUGHTS OF SOME WOMEN!

How do women answer this question once they have actually said it out loud? Here are some common responses:

"My body has let me down. I can't imagine why I can't keep going."

"Something is really wrong with me; I've always taken care of things in the past."

"People all over the world have larger problems than I do and they just handle it. What's wrong with me?"

"I don't want my spouse/partner/significant other to know that I've made this appointment. It would scare him/her to know I'm not coping."

"My mother had lots worse things in her life and she didn't need therapy."

"Other people get divorced/break up; lose their jobs; lose a loved one; can't decide what to do with their lives; or _____(your answer) and they don't end up in therapy – so what's my problem, anyway?

"This is just some luxury I don't need. (Or deserve). I'm being weak. I'm acting like a baby."

"I could use this money in a dozen different ways if I could just get hold of myself."

"People see me as someone who can handle anything. What would my family, my friends, my colleagues think of me if they knew I was doing this?"

"I couldn't stand to have my kids see me like this. I try to keep my feelings from showing when they're around."

"I've always been able to count on myself in a pinch. What does it mean that I can't seem to do it now?"

"Maybe I have a brain tumor!"

Strong words! And they are only representations of the thousands of other sentences that run around in women's heads. Hopefully, they demonstrate how a negative question mires you in self-doubt, shame, and blame. It heads you once again in the direction of self-doubt, blame and shame.

NOW, YOUR ANSWER

Take a few minutes right now and answer: "Why can't I cope with my problems by myself?" Let your thoughts flow onto the paper. Write everything you are aware of.

REMEMBER TO BE HONEST WITH YOURSELF! DON'T EDIT!

Review your answers and reflect on your physical and emotional reactions. For example: "I feel a tightness in my chest when I write these negative things about myself." or "I get scared just thinking about why I need help."

IS THERE A GOOD ANSWER TO A BAD QUESTION?

When you have become aware of the nagging negative question, "Why can't I cope with my problems by myself," answer immediately by saying. "I need help right now and it's okay".   Say it many times so you can feel a shift in your thinking and feeling. If it helps, write it down over and over.

Then expand your answer with the truth. "I need help right now and it's okay. I have problems and negative feelings I'm struggling with, (write them down) and I don't have to expect to handle them alone. Getting help is the smartest thing I can do."

REMEMBER TO REFRAME YOUR QUESTIONS

"Reframing" changes your focus and breaks through the negative energy that harms your sense of self worth.

As you practice reframing your negative questions you will notice subtle positive shifts in the way you think and feel. You'll begin feeling more clear, more focused on the specific problems you are confronting.

Now, clear your mind and reframe the question: "What are the circumstances – external and internal – that have brought me to this point of needing professional help?"

-Write down all the answers that come to you.

-Review your answers.

-Reflect on your thoughts and feelings. You might think: "After making this list, my thoughts are more clear." You might feel: "I'm scared but not as much as I was. It helps to get it on paper rather than just thinking about it all the time."

-Compare your thoughts and feelings to those in the "negative" question.

-Check for even subtle differences. Write them down.

WHAT MAKES ME ASK THESE NEGATIVE QUESTIONS?

The old ways of thinking are more familiar and consequently more powerful. They make change hard. The thinking you learned in childhood has become habitual. You may not even be aware you are doing it.

Each time you ask yourself a negative question, stop yourself and reframe it. Gradually your pattern of thinking and questioning yourself will begin to shift.

IF I ASK FOR HELP, IS THERE SOMETHING WRONG WITH ME?

Asking for help is actually a sign of strength. It means your system is too healthy to tolerate whatever is happening. The signs urging you to ask for help are positive. Your mind, body, emotions, or spirit (or all four) have "had it" with constant pressure and demands! Consequently, your "symptoms" may be coming from the healthy part of you, trying to get your full attention.

LISTEN TO YOUR BODY

Perhaps your body has signaled it's time to change behavior – with a symptom that frightens you – chest pains, heart palpitations, or a spastic colon. Perhaps the symptoms are emotional – difficulty getting through the day without having an angry outburst, or crying.

OBSERVE YOUR BEHAVIOR

Perhaps the signals have come from your behavior – you can't make decisions, can't concentrate, don't even want to take phone calls from close friends. Or maybe you feel rootless, empty and disconnected from anything important. These symptoms can feel overwhelming, but they all get your attention! And attention from you is just what your system needs!

A CONVERSATION WITH MY FOOT!

A few years ago I broke my right foot in what I viewed as a careless accident. For several days I was too angry and in too much pain to concentrate on the "message" my body was giving me. Finally, I decided to see if I could understand what was going on, other than the obvious inconveniences. I spent time relaxing and meditating and, honestly, having a conversation with my foot.

First, I "gave my foot a voice." I imagined what my broken foot would say if it could talk. I asked questions: What happened? What are you feeling? What do you need from me to heal?

The first message was pretty obvious. "You need to slow down." Doesn't take a genius or a psychologist to figure that one out! But as I continued, my foot said, "You are moving too fast to see the things you really need to see at this stage in your life." This got my attention! With more reflection, exploration and writing, I saw I was back in some of my old "workaholic" patterns – doing too much, and trying to do it all myself. My foot slowed me down long enough for re-evaluation, much needed goal setting, and the identification of the outside resources I needed to get me back on track.

TALKING TO YOURSELF IS REALLY OKAY

Experiment with welcoming these frightening but potentially helpful symptoms. Try: "My _____ (you fill in the symptom) is trying to tell me something. I need to pay attention and take care of myself. I need to listen, and I will get help if that's what I need." Now give your symptom a voice. See what it has to say! Ask it questions. Yes, have a conversation. Ask: What are you trying to tell me? Is there something you want me to do? And please pay attention even if it sounds silly!

Doing this exercise is hard when you're scared or in pain – or perhaps regard it as a stupid suggestion; however, it is possible to do and it does help.

YOU MAY NEED HELP TO IDENTIFY THE REAL PROBLEM

If you still believe the problem is you and your inability to do it yourself, consider the possibility that there are other things that aren't okay: 1) your decisions and choices; 2) your attitude or outlook; 3) the way you think; or 4) the negative sentences and questions running around in your head. If you are stuck in examining your defectiveness, you are paying attention to the wrong thing. You're not even working on the real problem.

THE COST OF DOING IT ALL ALONE: THE IMPACT ON SYDNEY

When this hard-working, high functioning and successful 40 year old woman called for an appointment, she said, "I know how busy you are, so if you don't have the time in your schedule for me I will understand. I really don't need to do this and I wouldn't want to take up your time if someone else really needs it. I can probably figure this all out by myself."

It took weeks to get her into the office because of her travel schedule. At first she talked about everyone but herself, regardless of my efforts to direct attention to her: "My friend Mary lost her husband in a tragic accident this year, and she's been back at work, getting on with her life just fine! And my colleague, John. No matter what difficulty he faces, nothing gets him down! They aren't in therapy, and they look just fine!"

FOCUSING ON THE WRONG PROBLEM

Sydney had convinced herself of two things: 1) she did not have a "real" problem; and 2) she should not be asking for help. This delayed identifying the true underlying issues causing her pain and unhappiness.

Sydney had always taken care of things by herself, and done so successfully. At least that was the way she saw herself, and judging from all the external measures of success, she was accurate. But she was also accurate when she said, my life is out of control."

Sidney was raised by members of her extended family when her 15-year-old mother couldn't cope. She learned to take care of herself early. She recalled sadly, "I knew I was an added burden, so I tried to do everything I could by myself. I was afraid if I asked for anything, I would put even more pressure on people."

She had stored up her feelings of pain, loss and anger. Now during the two years prior to calling for an appointment, her estranged mother had died; she had gone through a complicated and ugly divorce; she was struggling with her two children; she had increased her work demands by buying another company; and she was over-extended in her political and volunteer activities. Through all of this her baseline expectation was simple: "I can do this by myself."

This time Sydney's inability to ask for help was costing her far too much. She experienced chest and stomach pains, had severe anxiety attacks, couldn't sleep, couldn't concentrate, and couldn't calm the "demons" in her head. She was medicating herself with alcohol. Drinking was the only way she believed she could get to sleep. And regardless of the situation, she questioned: "Why can't I get a grip? I've always handled everything alone. *What* is wrong with me?!"

It took months before she trusted me enough to really commit to being helped. That shift began when she understood that her need for help did not mean she was a failure. She began to focus on the problems in her life rather than on her "defectiveness." She learned she was exhibiting strength by getting help, and that her old definition of being strong – sucking it up and keeping on," was not only inaccurate but was killing her

NECESSARY CHANGES

I helped Sydney focus on two basic goals – learning to trust people and ask for what she needed; and finding practical ways to take pressure off her life. She hired someone to clean her house – yes, she had been doing that too; she hired an assistant she had needed for well over a year. Together we examined every aspect of her work and personal schedule. A physical exam revealed an ulcer, so she stopped drinking and put together a healthier eating plan. She learned relaxation and meditation techniques. I referred her and her children for family therapy. She and I are still working on healing some of the old hurts from her childhood, and she is doing extremely well.

GETTING UNSTUCK USING PRODUCTIVE QUESTIONS

Sydney learned to ask herself healthy questions instead of constantly lamenting "Why can't I cope with my problems by myself?" Here are the questions she worked with.

HELP WANTED: KEY QUESTIONS

-How does it feel to ask for help?

-What scares me about asking for help?

-What is my experience in asking for help?"

-With my spouse/partner/significant other?

-With my parents or primary caretakers?

-With my friends?

-Who taught me I should do everything myself?

-Who are the positive examples in my life of people asking for help?

-In general, what have I learned about asking for help for *me*?

-Can I give myself permission to get the help I need?

-Write your answers. If the questions feel overwhelming, focus on them when you are ready.

"I am just a plain old failure! I can't do anything! I'm fat, and I'm always going to be fat. And I don't need your help in figuring that out!   This was a fairly common outburst from Izzie. She was still putting herself down for asking for help. After many weeks of writing down more rational, factual, and helpful ways of thinking, she began to make some changes. "I thought my big problem was not being able to lose weight! But the way I beat up on myself causes problems in every area of my life!"   Here's the set of statements she initially practiced writing and saying out loud.

"I have failed at losing the 10 pounds I want to lose. I am not a failure as a person. I am capable of losing 10 pounds if I eat three healthy meals a day, exercise, and continue to ask for help when I need it. This is hard work, sometimes I get discouraged and angry, but it is possible for me to reach my goal."

WHAT'S THE DIFFERENCE? IS IT SO IMPORTANT?

"I'm a failure" and "I failed to lose 10 pounds" are entirely different statements! "I am a failure" makes a statement about your very being. Just say it out loud a few times and experience the impact. You might feel your energy shift, feel negative emotions sweep through you – you might even start to feel depressed!

TRY IT YOURSELF

Experiment with the opposite statement: "I failed to _____." Insert something you were not able to do. Say this sentence out loud several times. This alternative statement is about a task, an event, a thing. You teach yourself to identify the failure to do a particular "thing" rather than calling yourself a failure.   You may still feel disappointed or let down; but you are less likely to feel overwhelmingly defeated and depressed.

IT REALLY DOES HELP

Healthy thinking and clarity about the real problem allows your mind to click into gear to problem solve. How can you change the situation, correct the mistake? You may still feel bad, but, hopefully, you aren't stuck in the belief that you, personally, are a failure. This is just one example of how your thinking and your belief structure – combined with the things you regularly tell yourself – may be the problem you need help with. Could you ask for help with that?

BE HEALTHY AND POWERFUL – ASK!

If you are always doing it by yourself, and always there for other people, you are probably pretty tired by now! You may have many of the physical, emotional, behavioral and spiritual symptoms described. Somewhere you learned that doing it yourself was the only safe, or practical, or right way. It might even have been the only way to survive. You feel more in control when you do it yourself. You feel a "superior" sense of power. But it's all backwards!

Healthy, powerful women ask for help. Think of the most powerful woman you know and admire. Imagine how she got where she is. Alone? Doubtful! Even Wonder Woman has a magic lariat! Remember the individual woman who comes to mind. If you are not talking to a family member, good friend, or a professional, you need a visual reminder to keep from isolating yourself.

When you persist in believing you are a failure because you can't fix it by yourself, you stay stuck. It takes real courage to look at what is really wrong in your life, give up blaming and beating up on yourself, and say, "It is really okay to ask for help. I deserve it." And you do!"

CHAPTER THREE

QUESTION THREE: WHAT IF PEOPLE KNEW WHAT I _REALLY_ THINK AND FEEL?

What a potent question! It speaks of fear and shame and amplifies the threat of exposing all the pain, disappointment and fear. It implies that certain thoughts and feelings define your true being and this "real you" is unacceptable and unlovable. It emphasizes the depth of women's isolation. Many women talk to no one about their deepest feelings.

BUT IF YOU REALLY KNEW.....

"What if people knew what I really think and feel?" See if it makes shivers go up and down your spine! But the question doesn't stop here. "What if you (including my therapist) find out the true and ugly nature of what I think about, the terrible feelings I have?" "Will you still like me or are my thoughts and feelings so sick and awful that you would not want to be my friend/spouse/partner/_____.

Many women repeat these questions in their minds, but don't have the courage to speak them. The fear of being rejected runs deep and strong. Airing your fears with an accepting and caring "witness" starts both a reality check and a healing process.

SECRETS AND LIES!

Long held secrets about what you think and feel loom as threats to your important relationships. "I can't tell him/her because _____ (you fill in the blank with your own damaging belief)."   It is lonely and sometimes terrifying to be isolated with thoughts or feelings that seem toxic. It is also unfair and unnecessary.

Many of the hidden "topics" are old. Things unspoken for so many years acquire an energy all their own – a potency that might have been relevant at the time of the event, but not today! However, if you have never spoken of such things, you may still believe they are bad and shameful. You may not understand that others might share your thoughts and feelings. The most helpful action is to talk to each other to understand the reality of shared thoughts and feelings. It is also the hardest thing to do. You have to move through layers of fear and shame. You have to see yourself honestly. And you must see others honestly.

The question itself, "What if people knew what I really think and feel" silences you, keeps secrets in place, and fuels their negative energy.

THE COMIC BOOK THIEF

When I was six, a twelve year old neighbor who sometimes supervised me for a few hours, taught me to steal comic books. Part of me knew I was doing something wrong, but I was easily influenced by an older girl I truly admired; and besides, I was getting free comic books! My mother caught me and told me I was a "bad girl" rather than a little girl with "bad behavior."

"Your behavior was so terrible we will never tell your father." Boy, that terrified me! I had ever seen my dad angry. So if he would be angry I knew I was very bad. Losing privileges to ride my bike was far less of a punishment than the thought of disappointing him.

For years, I never spoke of my "sins" to anyone. My secret grew in intensity as I told myself all the horrible things my behavior meant. As I progressed through adolescence, whenever I felt particularly bad about myself, I pulled out this secret and reminded myself of my lack of morals and good judgment. When I was 16, a friend told me she had gotten in trouble for shop lifting when she was 12. Just listening to her revelation sent a wave of hot fear running through me. I thought I would choke! But I didn't tell her about my career as a thief. I took only "secret comfort" in knowing a friend experienced something similar. Still I could not bring myself to share my own experience. My shame was so deeply ingrained I deprived myself of the relief that comes with sharing.

By the time I was in my 20's, I didn't think about the incident. However, in one of my early therapy sessions, I told the psychologist about stealing and found myself breaking down into a flood of tears. I was sweating, flushing, and having trouble breathing. I was so taken off guard by the intensity of my rcsponsc, I bccame even more overwhelmed and embarrassed! But I learned a powerful lesson – secrets, and the shame attached to them, are potent. As I continued my therapy, I reflected on more of the old, unspoken "bad things" about me. My list of things I was afraid for anyone to know turned out to be surprisingly long, but nothing on it was as earth-shattering as I had secretly expected.

FEAR OF FRAUD

Some women live in fear that they will be "found out."   "I am not really the good person you think I am." "I am not truly qualified for this job." "I'm not really as competent as I appear." You may fear you will ultimately encounter the person or the task that demonstrates you have somehow been getting by – magically! That you have feet made of clay. Your accomplishments don't count, or your character is deeply flawed. You wait for the moment when everyone will know who you really are – what you really think and feel.

HOW DID I LEARN MY TRUE THOUGHTS AND FEELINGS ARE BAD?

Consider this simple example of how we learn about our genuine thoughts and feelings.   Seven-year-old Lilly had an ugly fight with her best friend across the street. "Stomping mad," she ran into the house and slammed the front door. In seconds, her mother stood in her pathway, hands on hips, frowning disapproval.

"I can't believe you hit Sara Beth!" "She hit me first!" "Doesn't matter. Good little girls don't get mad. It's not nice." Lilly was crushed, consumed with the shame of disapproval, struggling with her feelings.

GETTING IT RIGHT

Like Lilly, you might say "I'm sorry, I didn't mean it"; admit being bad; and do whatever the adult tells you. You want to do whatever it is good little girls, nice little girls do. However, your internal response doesn't go away, even though you push it out of your awareness and stuff it somewhere.   It feels like it went away – temporarily.

WHAT ARE YOUR TRUE FEELINGS?

If you continually shift away from real or natural responses, you can develop a self, a "persona" you present to the world that is disconnected from the "core" of your authentic thoughts, feelings, and beliefs. You don't trust your full range of thoughts and feelings, and you don't learn to express anger, sadness, or disappointment appropriately. Instead you express a self that everyone around you seems to like. You, however, know you learned to keep the authentic part of you under wraps.

MY COPING MECHANISM

As a child, I was obsessed with pleasing the adults around me. The more people in authority responded with: "Linda, you are such a good girl!" "You are such a hard worker!" "You are so sweet!" the more I worked at behaving perfectly. I became an expert at figuring out what others expected. I was "hyper-vigilant." While I worked so hard on creating this perfect exterior, I lost the chance to experience my own reactions, to form my own solid opinions and beliefs.

In my teens and early 20's when asked what I thought, or felt or wanted, I often didn't know. I only knew what I believed I should think, feel, or want. My own preferences and opinions – even my deepest desires – were hidden under layers of denial.

MAYBE YOU WERE JUST THE OPPOSITE!

Perhaps your response was to rebel and do the opposite of what adults wanted. This behavior is also disconnected from what you really feel and think. It represents the opposite end of the same continuum – not being or becoming the person you want to be.

LOSING YOUR AUTHENTIC SELF

Regardless of which end of the continuum best describes you, your genuine thoughts and feelings do not go away. But the gap between the person you show to the world and the person you secretly believe yourself to be, can grow dramatically. As the gap increases, as your less authentic, pseudo self takes over, you feel more anxious about the difference. You believe that your "observable" self is not real because you know there's a secret self.

For example, you might be married with three children and secretly wish for a single life and a rewarding career instead. You might be divorced with a glamorous job, wishing to be married again, but embarrassed to say so. Perhaps you always date men and know that you prefer women. You may have survived a childhood so ugly you believe no one could accept it as the truth so you never speak of it. Maybe you have a reputation for being outspoken but never say all of what you really think.

HOW DID THE "SECRET" GET SO POWERFUL?

None of these differences (secrets) mean you are a bad person, but they sometimes feel too risky to share. However, keeping parts of the self hidden inhibits self expression, and fuels the sense of doubting almost everything you do express.

The secret self becomes "encased" in feelings of shame. Shame surges through the body and mind, disconnecting you from others and from yourself. The disconnect between the two selves, as well as the disconnect between you and others, can make both your "selves" feel shaky. But both parts of the self are real.

Life can seem fraudulent or about to "unravel" when you are disconnected from some of your genuine feelings, thoughts or beliefs. Finding out what is real and what isn't begins with learning about the hidden parts and then sharing with someone you can trust. Many women hold on to secrets and struggle with the courage to speak them.

WHICH PART OF ME DO I TRUST?

For most women, the hidden secrets feel more real. You live with them all the time, in your head, so they accumulate negative energy. But the "nice" parts you show the world, those that feel "fraudulent," are more real than you believe. Once you accept and connect all the aspects of your unique self, you can begin to trust who you are. Once you trust yourself, being and expressing that self becomes easier. The hard part is taking that first step.

WHAT ABOUT YOU?

Take a minute to pay attention to the "secrets" you have been reflecting on just while reading these last few paragraphs. Ask yourself, "What if people knew what I really think and feel?

-Write your responses quickly.

-Be honest with yourself. Don't edit.

-Check to see what you feel physically and emotionally. Record your responses.

-Now write some of the things you are afraid to share with another person. If you are afraid to put them on paper, review them in your mind.

(Later, when you are ready, it will help you to write them.)

-Once again, check to see what you feel physically and emotionally.

-Make notes of what you feel. For example, "My body is tense all over when I think about these things." "I'm terrified to put these things on paper. I can't!"

WHAT DO OTHER WOMEN SAY?

Here are some of the self destructive answers women have for the question, the ones that don't help:

-You would know just how crazy and insecure I am.

-It would disappoint you to hear what is in my head.

-You would be afraid that I am a bad mother!

-You wouldn't want to be my therapist….my friend/spouse/partner/lover.

-You'd want to put me in a hospital.

-I know you say it's okay to talk about it, but I can't make myself do it!

-Will you promise not to leave if I tell you?

-I'll lose my job.

-My husband/partner will leave me.

-I live a lie. How can I face that.

-I'll die if I tell.

PATTERNS! WHAT DO THEY MEAN?

By now you are probably noticing a pattern of thinking unfolding.   If so many women think and feel similarly, it must mean something about our "systems" – our relationships, families, schools, churches, and work settings. It lets you know that part of the problem is "outside you."

REFRAMING .. AND WHEN THE QUESTION STAYS STUCK IN MY BRAIN????

"What if people really knew.....? This old and deep rooted question is like a dandelion, popping up again and again. When the question plagues you, when the shame silences you, try these answers. Then develop your own.

"Everyone has negative or frightening thoughts sometimes. I am not alone with what I think and feel. I will discover that as I talk about myself."

"Having negative or frightening thoughts and feelings does not mean I am a bad person. Not being able to talk about them means I isolate myself and increase my level of anxiety."

"Some of my thoughts and feelings sound ugly/mean/unloving/ungrateful/unkind/ too hard to deal with (you add your own best description). I don't share them with anyone because I worry that people would think less of me. My negative thoughts and feelings need to be examined, not hidden away. I can learn to understand them. I can write about them and talk about them in a safe place with a safe person. Then I'll feel better than I do right now."

"Sharing my scary thoughts and feelings will be hard, but I can do it if I ask for help. I deserve help from friends and family and if I need it, from professionals."

"Facing some of the things in my mind may mean I will need to make some big changes. I can change gradually; I don't have to fix everything at once."

MAYBE I SHOULD STOP QUESTIONING MYSELF ALTOGETHER!

 Before you worry about questions in general, remember this a process of reflection. Questioning yourself is healthy when you learn it is essential to ask productive questions. Keep this question to use, for any subject, when you are working on reframing: "What is the worst thing that could happen to me if _____."

Here, the question is "What is the worst thing that could happen to me if I told a safe person what I really think and feel?" This approach helps you dig out all the negative thoughts in your head – and then, eventually challenge them.

-Write all your responses.

-Review what you have written and pay close attention to your physical and emotional response. You will still have intense feelings; however, they are more likely to be real, not exaggerated.

-Compare your thoughts and feelings with those from the "negative" question.

-Check for any subtle differences and write them down. When you identify genuine feelings, you can work with those feelings, moving yourself in the direction of healing and changing.

IT'S NOT AS BAD AS THE WAY YOUR THINKING MAKES IT

No matter how negative your thoughts are, telling them to someone who is safe will not kill you. You will have to confront pain. That can take some time and usually, if your fear is intense, it demands some professional help. Withholding your thoughts and feelings becomes a survival tool. You are unlikely to "let go" of behaviors that have made you feel safe unless you believe there is an equally powerful way to protect yourself.

CHALLENGE YOUR BELIEFS

Sometimes getting a more realistic picture of what is in your mind and heart can help make things less scary. Writing down your fears helps put them into perspective. If you believe that no one would like you or love you if they knew your true thoughts and feelings, give yourself permission to challenge that belief. If you are ready, answer these questions.

-What authentic thoughts and feelings seem so terrible to you? See if you are ready to write some of them down on paper. If it feels too scary, wait and try again later. If you are concerned someone will read what you write, burn your notes over the kitchen sink. At some point it is important for you to write, even if you have to rent a safety deposit box for privacy!

- Make a list of the specific things you fear. Start with one secret. Then see if others come to the surface.

- Make a list of the people you fear. Identify, if you know, what it is about each person that frightens you.

-Think about one or two important people in your life. What would you most like to tell that person about what you think and feel?

REFLECTION

Review all the things you have written or reflected on while reading. Is there is any shift in your belief about how terrible your thoughts and feelings are?

GETTING TO KNOW YOU

So far I have yet to know a person who isn't concerned about sharing certain thoughts and feelings. But stuffing such thoughts and feelings becomes damaging to you, to others, and to your relationships. The emotions fester and gain energy through lack of expression. Acknowledging, accepting and working with your secret thoughts and feelings will diffuse them and make them less overwhelming. Think of them as needing to be metabolized! If you eat too much fatty ice cream and don't exercise enough to burn it off, it is almost guaranteed to attach to some part of your body!

PAY ATTENTION TO WHAT SCARES YOU – DO A REALITY CHECK

It is normal to be anxious about things you have never shared with anyone. Acknowledge the fear, be gentle with yourself, and consider submitting your fears to a reality test. Pick the safest person you know, and share one of your less scary secrets.

Pay attention to how if feels to talk about a secret fear, to the response you get, and to how you feel at the end of the conversation. If you are happy with the outcome, consider sharing even more. If you don't like the results, wait until you feel stronger, then try again. Perhaps try with a different person. If you can't do it yet that's okay. Instead, do something totally different.

Ask a safe person "What is the very worst thing anyone has ever shared with you?" Now check your own level of judgment. Often the reason you are so afraid of being judged is because you are so quick to judge and criticize others. Fear is heightened by your knowledge of your own response. You may be surprised and relieved to learn that other people are more forgiving and understanding than you are!

You may, on the other hand, be much more tolerant of others than of yourself. Ask, "Where did I learn to be so hard on myself? Or, "When did this severe self-judgment and criticism of myself or others begin?" These questions can help you understand how long your pattern has been in place. And once you understand it you can change.

KIM'S STRUGGLE

Despite individual therapy, Kim still believed she was the only person around with "bad thoughts and feelings." I knew she needed to share with other women, but she resisted joining a group. She couldn't risk "exposing" herself to the judgment of others. Gradually, after six months of hard work in therapy, Kim felt strong enough to trust my recommendation and try a group. She was terrified! But even the first session made a difference.

WHAT HAPPENED? WHAT WAS THE GROUP LIKE?

When a new person joined a group, I asked the current members to introduce themselves. They share information on the family they grew up in, their current home and work situations, and they describe the problems they are solving in group. Just listening to seven other "normal" women talk about their problems made Kim realize that she wasn't alone:

Janet: "When I came to group I was convinced I would never feel good again because I couldn't ask for help. I couldn't talk to anyone about my life. I've learned to talk about my fears – I am afraid I am a bad mother. I never hit my kids, but I think about it. I was beaten as a   child, so I was terrified my thoughts made me just like my parents."

Amy: "I thought I hated my husband. I had such horrible thoughts about him, I considered getting a divorce, but I never talked about it, not even to my best friend. Therapy has helped me sort through my feelings. I'm finding out what the real problems are, learning to separate them from the ones I made up. We're in couples therapy and we are doing better.

As the other members shared, Kim's body relaxed. After a few more weeks of group, she asked the members if they had "secrets" they were embarrassed about. One or two of the women laughed and talked about their fears. Kim wasn't ready to reciprocate but that day she became a part of the group, knowing she could talk there, and no one would think she was terrible.

MOVING ON

The thoughts and feelings you hesitate to share do not make you bad, but they do make you feel bad. They may also lead you into behaviors that are negative and destructive. Talk, talk, talk; but choose carefully with whom. And if sharing still feels like too much to ask, write, write, write. As you learn that others have similar thoughts and feelings and have made their lives better, you'll see that change is possible!

CHAPTER FOUR

QUESTION FOUR: WHAT IF I LOSE CONTROL – START TO CRY OR GET ANGRY AND CAN'T STOP?

One of the largest myths is that women have permission to express feelings! You indeed can emote – cry at movies, or show concern over spouses, partners, children and pets. But few people want to hear you or see you when you voice your intense, important feelings. And losing control, or getting angry is unfeminine, scary to the receiver, and a sure sign you are crazy!

LOSING CONTROL IS FRIGHTENING!

If you have been "holding on" to anger and pain for many years, in response to these prohibitions, it is definitely scary to contemplate letting it go. Some of the fear comes from inside you, and some is generated from the anticipated response from others.

TAKING CONTROL VS BEING IN CHARGE

Instead of "holding on" all the time – trying so hard to be in control – consider "letting go" and being in charge! It may not sound different, but it is. Here's one example of how it works.

STEP ONE

Take a deep breath and hold it for as long as you can. As you hold your breath, close your eyes tightly. Tense your muscles and hold the posture for as long as possible. When you can't hold your breath any longer, release your breath and try to let go of the tension you've created in your body.

When you hold your breath and tighten your muscles, you are replicating what automatically happens when you try to "control."

When you feel "out of control," you hold on to try to regain control either of yourself, someone else, or some hoped for outcome. Holding on constricts and diminishes all dimensions of the self.

-Your mind is tight/closed and you can't think as clearly.

-You can't feel your body with accuracy. It is knotted up.

-Your emotions aren't accessible. You have slammed a lid on them.

-The spiritual dimension of the self is closed.

This is the "state" you produce when you are trying to be in control!

STEP TWO

Now take a long, deep breath, open your eyes, and focus on relaxing, releasing tension. Take another deep breath and relax just a little bit more. Smile, even if you don't feel like smiling. Let your self feel and observe the difference. If it helps, repeat the process, paying attention to any small changes you notice – emotionally and physically.

RELAX, LET GO, PAY ATTENTION, AND YOU'RE IN CHARGE!

Being in charge is exactly the opposite of being in control. It is about breathing, relaxing, letting go, and paying attention.

When you breathe, relax, and let go, you think more clearly, identify your emotions, pay attention to your body's signals, and clear the pathway to your spiritual self.

In this "state of awareness" or "mindfulness" you can make decisions and choices, and impact or influence people and outcomes. And you can do so from a centered, healthy place.

If the difference doesn't make much sense, take some time to think about it. Control "addiction" – the on-going persistence to hold on to what you think and feel and want – to make others think, feel, do or believe what you want them to, without ever telling them directly, can be so habitual that you are unaware of it until you feel both physically and emotionally ill.

I CAN MAKE THIS WORK MY WAY!

The need to be in control is well ingrained. Most people believe it is a worthy goal to attempt to "control" their own feelings, thoughts, and behaviors, as well as the feelings, thoughts and behaviors of others. They further believe it is definitely important to try to control outcome. With such a common set of beliefs, the idea of shifting to "being in charge" feels complex.

CONTROL YOURSELF!!

Control is Impossible ! In spite of this reality, many people become control addicts – obsessing and focusing unnecessary energy on shutting down their own thoughts and feelings, and trying to do the same to others.

Women are particularly susceptible to control addiction. The fear of losing control grows after years of holding on to feelings and thoughts judged as inappropriate or unacceptable while holding back what you do feel. Judgment, being told what is "right" to feel, what you "should" feel, sends the powerful and negative message: Control yourself!

THE DREADFUL DUO – ANGER AND PAIN

Anger and pain are the two most powerful emotions women are trying to keep under wraps. No one wants to see or talk to an angry woman! And for heaven's sake don't let anyone see you in pain. Keep a stiff upper lip! Reinforce that "nice girl" image you acquired so long ago. Smile, be pleasant, smooth things over; and see if you can make everyone and everything okay. Except, of course, yourself!

If you don't control your anger and pain, you will end up in a conflict that's dangerous, because in honest conflict, authentic anger and pain may surface. Consequently holding on becomes the only solution. You learned to do it a long time ago to survive.

AM I CONTROLLING? JUST ASK _____!

Just in case you believe you aren't addicted to control or at least on a quest for control, consider this example. I am very direct about asking for what I want – well, most of the time! Recently I asked a male friend to take me to an early morning flight.

I made my request, and he said, "Yes."

BUT, I DON'T LIKE THE WAY YOU SAID THAT!

But I didn't like the way he said yes. He "muttered" under his breath, looked irritated, changed his body language and voice tone, and sent a considerable amount of other negative non-verbal messages! Watching him, and diligently listening to him, I realized a ride to the airport was not all I wanted. If I had been requesting only transportation, I would have accepted his agreement and gone about my business. But I didn't walk away. Why? Because in addition to wanting a ride to the airport, I wanted him to want to go ! I wanted him to like it ! And I wanted him to have fun on the way!

Even that embarrassing recognition wasn't enough, because I then proceeded to try to talk him into feeling and thinking the way I wanted him to! Eventually I realized that I had let my old control needs hook me. I wanted to feel more connected, and I tried, unsuccessfully, to control his thoughts and feelings in order to do so.

When I share this example of my own "addiction to control" in workshop settings, waves of laughter flow across the room. One participant said she calls that "orchestrating" not controlling. Call it what you want, but recognize it throws you, the other person, and the relationship off track.

CAN THIS HURT ME?

Control efforts like this are exhausting. They don't work; they cause tension and conflict; and your frustration can make you try harder at the very thing causing you difficulty. Trying to control can damage the relationships you genuinely care about and harm your physical, emotional, intellectual and spiritual health.

WOMEN'S EXPRESSIONS OF THEIR FEARS

Some of the things women say when they face being out of control reveal the fear as well as the damage that has already been done:

"If I let myself cry I'm afraid I won't stop."

"Crying just makes me sick to my stomach! I don't want to start because I'm afraid I'll throw up."

"I have to go to work today, I can't cry and go around with no make up on."

"I'm afraid of what's down in there."

"The crazy thing is I don't know what I am crying about."

"I'm afraid my anger is so intense that I would hurt myself."(or you)

"I don't think you could handle my anger."

"If I get angry or cry, I know you will leave."

"I shouldn't be angry unless I know what I am angry about."

"I know I'll lose my mind, go crazy."

"I'll disappear!"

WHAT IS YOUR ANSWER?

Now answer "What if I lose control – start to cry or get angry and can't stop?" for yourself.

-Write as many thoughts as you can quickly. Be honest with yourself

-Don't edit.

-Put down whatever comes into your mind.

-Review your answers and reflect on your physical and emotional

reactions. For example, "I know I can't really let go. It scares me too much."

I DIDN'T REALIZE WOMEN WERE SO AFRAID

It makes sense to fear deep emotions you have never fully expressed. You probably learned a long time ago to stay in control. Some of you are successful up to a point, then you lose it, cry and don't understand what you're crying about or explode inappropriately. Some of you manage to never get really angry or tearful but are often depressed, anxious, or physically ill. Holding on takes a toll. Here is a metaphor to help you understand it in more detail.

THE FEMALE TRASH COMPACTOR

Imagine that you have a large trash compactor in your body. It fills the trunk of your body. The base rests on your pelvic bone, the opening at your throat. By age 30, most of you have this container nearly full. Each time you avoid expressing anger or pain, you put the feeling in the compactor. It has to go somewhere! You use the same container when you are unable to voice positive feelings – joy, love, and self worth. The trash compactor also holds your unexpressed thoughts. Ideas, preferences, opinions held back – for whatever reasons you tell yourself you can't express them – are layered in the trunk of your body.

LEARNING TO USE THE COMPACTOR

As a woman you learn to be understanding and receptive in your intimate relationships – to put the needs of others first. Yours are not as important. Over the years, and out of your awareness, you store away those unexpressed needs, and all those hard to voice beliefs and thoughts and feelings. You begin to experience overload. Your compactor is dangerously full. You may feel emotional rushes of anxiety or tension. Some women describe the sensation of a washing machine agitator in their solar plexus and chest. To control such uncomfortable feelings, to "compact the trash," you typically quit breathing, swallow hard, count, or attempt to push your mind into a rational thought process, giving you the illusion of being "back in control."

ADDITIONAL TECHNIQUES FOR COMPACTING TRASH

As unexpressed feelings accumulate, there is just not enough room in the trash compactor. To cope some women use alcohol, drugs, or food to quiet the persistent rumble of unacceptable feelings or thoughts. Some find relief through excessive TV viewing, spending too much money, gambling, working long hours, sexual acting out, or escaping into another bad relationship.

THE RESULTS OF A FULL TRASH COMPACTOR

Finally, no matter how hard you try to compact the trash, there is just no more room, and the results can be:

-An angry, emotional outburst, far out of proportion to the event

-A tendency to be tearful or cry easily, especially when someone says something nice or nurturing to you, or when you see an emotionally provocative movie or television show.

-Ongoing irritability – everything and everyone is annoying.

-Physical symptoms of some severity such as ulcers, gastritis or colitis, heart palpitation, muscle spasms, headaches.

-Frequent physical illness such as colds or flu that require bed rest and medication.

An angry outburst, a good cry, a few unfair, sarcastic remarks, or a few days in bed will often clean out about one third of the trash compactor contents. You may be left with the concern that your feelings and behaviors were extreme or out of proportion. "Why was I that angry?" "Why did I feel so sad?" Regardless, with relief of tension, you can return to routine behavior until the trash compactor fills up once again.

THIS FEELS FAMILIAR!

The process creates a vicious cycle. The repetition of filling up and then partially "unloading" blocks the feelings you need to express. And as you continue to feel "in and out of control," you may question "what's wrong with you?" and feel just a little bit crazy. Self doubt leads to even more holding on, more efforts to control unexpressed emotions. No wonder you feel so bad! What you have traditionally called out of control, maybe even crazy, is "overload." Your trash compactor is too full!

SOME OF US ARE PRECOCIOUS!

Sometimes I think my trash compactor was full by the time I was 10! Tears were not "modeled" or "allowed" in my family. I don't remember ever see anyone cry, even at funerals. And I don't remember hearing either of my parents express anger. Disappointment, disapproval, criticism, but not straight forward anger. Thankfully, from elementary school through college, I had the important outlet of athletics. In a series of structured activities – basketball, softball, volleyball, and track I had permission to hit and kick and yell. When I reflect back on my life, I wonder if I would have survived without these experiences which provided so much necessary release and at the same time built my sense of self-worth.

DON'T YOU DARE CRY

One thing, however, was missing. Athletes definitely didn't cry. I did not shed a tear when I had three vertebra knocked out of place in a basketball game or hit my head dozens of time on a hard concrete court. I think we sometimes cried after a big loss but only in the safety and privacy of the locker room.   Affirmation came from pretending I was okay. And I learned to control accumulated pain and grief. By the time I entered graduate school, the accumulated feelings of loss, disappointment, and plain old normal sadness were stuck inside me, and any release was my quick and usually inappropriate responses of anger.

It took years for me to finally feel safe enough to let go of so many old stored up feelings. The fear that no one would be able to handle them was powerful. My eventual healing started when I participated in a month long workshop with 20 other professional women. I found a therapist I trusted enough to begin to express my feelings. It changed my life to unload my trash compactor.

HOW DO I KEEP FROM FILLING IT BACK UP?

To start the process of cleaning out your own trash compactor, ask yourself, "What if I lose control – start to cry or get angry and can't stop?"

-Write until you believe you have no more responses left.

-Be honest with yourself. Don't edit.

-Pay attention to how you feel, physically and emotionally.

-Write anything!

REMEMBER TO REFRAME IT

"What are the things, the people, the events in my life that contribute to my intense fears of expressing my feelings?"

-Again, write your answers quickly.

-Be honest. Don't edit.

-Check to see what you feel physically and emotionally.

-Write anything!

-Compare your reactions to those from the negative question.

By now you can probably see subtle shifts in your thoughts and feelings when you reframe a question. Once you have made a question more productive, you are much more likely to understand your reality – internally and externally. Changing the question doesn't make it easy. It defines, realistically, what you are struggling to change and heads you in a new direction.

EXPLORING ANGER AND PAIN

Examine your fears and anxieties in a healthy, safe way by answering these additional questions.

-What am I angry about?

-Who am I angry with?

-What situations in my life feel painful?

-When I feel pain, who are the people I think about?

-What do I think and feel when I consider expressing my pain and anger?

-Do these feelings of anger and pain have a long history?

-What would it be like to find a safe place and a safe person and begin to learn to let go of these feelings?

I KNOW I'LL ASK THIS QUESTION FOR A LONG TIME!

When the negative question and all the bad answers stay "stuck" in your brain, remember the image of the trash compactor, and try these answers:

"I am afraid of the intensity of my anger and my pain. I know I need someone to help me understand it and express it. I can ask a friend/family member/_____ to help me find good professional help."

"Maybe I can learn to trust my feelings regardless of how intense they are."

"I will need to feel safe to start this process. That is a legitimate need."

"Many people have told me I have a horrible temper, so I need to learn to express anger appropriately."

"Bad things have happened to me, and my feelings are appropriate. However they overwhelm me and I will need help with them.

MARY BETH'S CONFLICT

Mary Beth had been in therapy off and on over the years and believed she was basically okay. However, she came to her first appointment with me stating, " I'm going to burst or explode! One day I feel fine, the next I want to scream or punch something." She had become afraid that she would hurt someone. In reality she was a tiny, gentle woman who never even raised her voice.

AN INTENSIVE FORM OF THERAPY

After we had worked together for several weeks, I suggested she participate in an "Intensive". In this week long experience, six to eight individual participants work with two therapists who create a safe environment to understand, release and heal feelings that produce this level of fear and anxiety.

For the first two days Mary Beth politely watched others work. Her participation was respectful, but guarded. However, when she saw another woman with a background similar to hers – an abusive childhood followed by two abusive, alcoholic marriages — safely and productively express her anger and pain with our help, she was willing to try. Mary Beth cried and yelled for over an hour while we sat with her, kept her safe, and guided her energy towards healing, problem solving, and resolution. For another two hours she role played conversations with her parents and her husbands, making both emotional and cognitive connections about the feelings that had been so confusing to her for so many years.

FIGURING IT OUT – FINALLY!

Mary Beth discovered that if she expressed and understood her feelings rather than holding on to them, she didn't have to live with fear of what she felt. She trusted herself for the first time in many years. By the end of the week, following hours of hard work, she said: "It hurt like hell, but I'm just not afraid of myself now. It is hard to tell you what freedom that is for me. It's like I have been a prisoner in my own mind, and now I'm not!"

ONE FINAL CONFESSION......

She also told the woman who had worked before her: "I was convinced you were much crazier than I was, so when you didn't scare the therapists I knew I would be okay!"

MAKING YOUR UNDERSTANDING WORK FOR YOU

It's normal to experience anxiety when you consider expressing your feelings. So if you think it's because you are crazy or exaggerating or just unable to "get a grip," see if you can consider this instead: the anxiety may have accumulated during the years of a difficult relationship or unsatisfactory job. And it may reach all the way back to your childhood. Your bad feelings intensify when a current situation triggers old memories or "old unresolved issues." You feel them as if they are happening right now! When old feelings "merge" with current feelings, that connection can be powerful enough to overwhelm and frighten you.

MAUREEN'S EXPERIENCE

Maureen described this experience in group. She was an "expert" at holding on and stuffing her trash compactor; but she was struggling to understand what caused her occasional angry outbursts. She recounted her last fight with her husband.

THEIR DIALOGUE

"I said to Will: 'I'm angry with you!' I remember feeling proud of myself for saying that directly and fairly calmly. I felt hot and agitated. I was restless and edgy, but I felt I was doing it right for a change."

He shot back at me: "I don't have time for your bullshit right now. Get off my back!"

CONSCIOUSNESS FOR MAUREEN

"When he said that, something inside me snapped. At first it was like water breaking through a damn. I felt all this energy surge through me – and I was filled with my anger towards him. I was frightened because I knew I could hit him. Plus it didn't make sense to be so upset by this conversation."

"Will said: ' Maureen, what's wrong with you?'"

"By now I wasn't listening to him. My mind had told me to hold on to my feelings and warned me of all the horrible, ugly things that would happen if I let my feelings out. And my feelings were so intense and out of proportion to the situation, I didn't have to think about stuffing it. I just shut my anger down.

I could tell most of the anger was old. Some of it was from lots of unresolved fights with Will; but even more was from all those lost arguments with my Dad. It was like watching old silent movies in my head – pictures of fights with Dad and Will kept flashing. I didn't get to say what I needed to say to Will, but I didn't blow up either. And this time I was conscious of the process from start to finish. I could feel it

70

was both physical and emotional. And I could hear the sentences in my big old left brain! I really think this is progress!"

WHAT HAPPENED?

Maureen was accurate about her progress. For months she had tried to understand the conflict between wanting to express feelings and at the same time being afraid to do so because they never came out "right." In this encounter with her husband, she felt the power of old feelings – how they overwhelmed her, blocking clear thinking and communication.

Equally important, Maureen felt the power of her negative thoughts. She believed that "horrible, ugly" outcomes resulted from expressing feelings. These convictions were strong enough to shut down all that physical and emotional energy! The change for her was consciousness. She finally saw what she was doing. She felt and observed what happened in her body. She listened to the messages in her head. As a result she worked on saying what she needed to say, doing what she needed to do, safely and constructively.

YOUR INTERNAL "AGITATOR" CAN QUIET DOWN

Opposing forces are at work when your feelings try to come out, and your mind tries to stop them. One energetic force acts against another – your body possesses a true understanding of the power and healing in breathing, releasing, letting go, and experiencing the moment – your mind expresses the fear, the warnings of frightening outcomes if you do release. The "battle" can feel like an internal "collision" – an anxiety attack, panic attack, or deep depression.

The intensity makes letting go, releasing in a natural and normal way look impossible. Holding on feels more normal, safe. Consequently, trust in the process for that first step to let go is essential. A safe person, a therapist experienced in this deeper level of work creates the space needed until you learn to trust your body.

The more intense your feelings, the more likely they are connected to historic or earlier life or childhood events. The more frightened you are of your feelings the more important it is to get help. And you deserve help. If you share what is going on with one safe person, you may be able to clarify what you need to get your life going in a healthier, productive direction.

Is it hard at first? Yes. Can you learn to trust yourself? Yes. Maureen's consciousness helped her build trust in herself. She was less fearful when her feelings made sense.

Remember it is your life and you can take the necessary steps to assure it is the life you want. Let go, and give it a try!

CHAPTER FIVE

QUESTION FIVE: "WHAT IF I LOOK INSIDE AND THERE IS NOTHING THERE OR I HATE WHAT I FIND?"

When I was 21 I moved to the East Coast to teach English in a college prep boarding school. I had graduated with honors, served as president of my sorority, been selected Missouri's Young Career Woman, won a national public speaking contest in Washington, D.C. and completed an exciting summer job with the Department of Labor's Neighborhood Youth Corps. I was doing almost "everything right" and likely rather "full of myself." Consequently I was speechless when a new friend and teaching colleague took me aside and said: "Linda, you can be one of the most superficial people I have ever known. Sometimes I don't think you know who you are."

We were leaving a reception following a recital where we entertained parents, guests, and visiting city dignitaries – something I considered myself quite good at doing!

I was devastated! I didn't know how to respond; I didn't even know what she meant! After all, I was "Little Miss Perfect" and working hard at it. I assumed someone as successful as I was – at least so far – surely must know herself! But I began questioning and exploring. I really had no option!

A NEW VIEW OF MYSELF

I discovered there was a great deal I didn't know about myself, and I realized I was a little uneasy, even a little afraid of that unknown. I had spent most of my life being pleasing, knowing what others wanted from me. I was skilled at identifying and then accomplishing many of the external markers of success for young women. I was education, career, and goal oriented – a little less traditional than many of my female peers. I wanted to succeed, "be liked" and have fun! And most of the time, up to that point, my success was affirmed, not challenged. Certainly not deeply examined by me!

That confrontation with my friend started a process that changed my career direction as well as my life. It was painful and shameful, but eventually I was grateful to her.

AN ANXIOUS LOOK INSIDE

Five years later, as an intern in a University counseling center, I certainly understood when my client, Angela said: "Sometimes I think there is no one home inside me." Dozens of other women clients expressed different versions of the same concern: "I am nobody." "What if the person I really am is not worth knowing?" The questions in their minds, similar to the ones I had asked myself, were potent in their negativity: "What if I look inside and there is nothing there?" "What if I hate what I find?

My own anxious search for the "real or deeper me" during my four years of graduate school became an adventure in self exploration – knowing and liking myself from the inside out – and created a foundation for understanding the questions.

BUT THESE ARE TWO VERY DIFFERENT QUESTIONS

These questions, as different as they appear, are actually at opposite ends of the same continuum of self-defeating inquiry. You may believe both things about yourself. One minute you are empty, worthless, the next you are full of unlikeable qualities.

These two "what if" questions sound logical if you are confused or fearful about who you are. You may discover you don't know yourself – even when you feel confident about your insights into your spouse, partner, kids, good friends, mother, boss or employees! If you are an "emotional maintenance worker" you have learned to focus your attention and energy on understanding others. This leaves you insufficient time and energy to focus on yourself.

THE FEAR COMES FROM DOING IT THE WAY SOMEONE ELSE WANTS YOU TO

The institutions in our society provide positive reinforcement when you give your attention to relationships. It helps to remember that from an early age you were taught to connect to others and nurture relationships. The connections are essential in your role identification in our culture —you are defined as a daughter, sister, mother, wife, partner. You are taught, and you learn well, to know the people around you. You are taught less frequently to know yourself.

Not knowing yourself can create depression and anxiety. It is expressed by women with exaggerated thoughts like these:

"Sometimes I feel so empty I just know there is nothing inside me to discover."

"There is an ugly black hole in me and I don't want to know what's in it."

"I have no idea what I want or really like. Ask me what my favorite food is and I can tell you my husband's – not mine!"

"How can I make a decision about school/a job when I don't even know what interests me?"

"Sometimes I don't think I'm really interested in anything – when I look inside I see nothing! And I don't want to do anything except sit and look out the window. See, I am worthless, lazy!"

"I get glimpses of this mean, really evil part of me. It scares me. I don't want to explore that."

"It feels like trying to start a car without gas. There is nothing in me."

"I tried to find my "inner child" in a workshop and didn't see anything. I was too afraid to tell the workshop leader, but it scares me to death that I can't find myself."

"I don't see how this therapy can help because I don't know if I really want to know myself – I don't trust who I might be."

"What if I don't like who I become when I learn to take care of myself? I will probably just turn out to be a selfish bitch!"

"I've never made a decision for myself. EVER! How can I learn to trust myself to do it this late in life?"

"I grew up in a strict Catholic family, then a convent. When I was over 40 I made my first independent decision – I bought a coat by myself with my own money. See what I mean. I'm afraid I have no idea who I am and what I want to do and it sends shivers up my spine."

"I tried to journal last night like you suggested. I have nothing to write. I can't do it. There is nothing in me. I have nothing to say."

"When I meditate at home, I see nothing but this blackness in me. I know that's all there really is."

"When my real self emerges here in your office, you'll see how boring I really am." (or worthless, or bad, or ugly, or dumb)

FEAR KEEPS YOU STUCK

These are painful and frightening thoughts. They serve as powerful roadblocks to your process of self-discovery. Encouragement to question yourself feels too risky because you don't know what you will find. You don't know how you will feel about what you find.

Fear is intensified by the reality of the trash compactor. Once you understand there is possibly a "stockpile" of unexpressed feelings, unloading it, even to examine the deep and wonderful aspects of who you are, is likely more intimidating. The external orientation – energy directed towards the thoughts, feelings, needs and preferences of others – keeps you from asking yourself: What do I think? Feel? Need? Prefer? Value? Care about? Want to do with my life?

Unloading the trash compactor can help you answer the questions but the fear of asking keeps the trash compactor full and the fear of emptiness or that you will hate what you find intensifies.

SUE ANN'S CONFLICT KEPT HER STUCK

After seeing several therapists Sue Ann said didn't understand her, she started therapy with me. It was hard to understand her because her fear paralyzed her when she talked about herself. We took baby steps for a long time.

After several sessions focused on her history, her family background, and building as safe an environment as possible with her, I gave her an assignment: "tell me one thing about yourself that makes you uncomfortable." She came in ready to discuss her dislike of her appearance, making clear she did not fully understand the question was intended as internal – something about challenging feelings or thoughts. We had to back up and go even more slowly.

I focused on examples of thoughts, feelings, fears of previous clients similar to the ones you've read, and asked her to relate to them if she could. That opened a door inside her – slightly. It also exaggerated a tightness, a physical stiffness and holding on. Slowly we worked with breathing, getting comfortable with allowing more than shallow breathing while she talked. I taught her to meditate but for weeks she was only comfortable doing it in the office with me. The physical work helped but she continued to say: "I can't talk about my feelings if they are buried in the trash compactor. They might swallow me up."

Things turned in a dramatic new direction when she reported an intense argument with her mother. Sue Ann's anger intensified and her body began to shake. She was unable to control movement in her arms and legs. I quickly sat next to her and with permission, put one hand on her back between her shoulder blades and the other firmly in her solar plexis, coaching her on breathing and allowing the feelings out. Slowly, she collapsed into deep sobs.

I continued coaching her through the release for about 15 minutes. She was exhausted, but safe. The difference in her body astonished her. We worked for about three more sessions understanding what had happened – the content, the connections to her past and her present. She began to truly trust her body – her feelings and her thoughts. Her work on understanding herself and moving forward with her life began with confidence.

COULD I DO THAT? DO I NEED TO DO THAT?

Everyone brings a different and specific need to therapy. At the same time, many find similar patterns with other women, and that can ease some of the anxiety about feeling so different. Regardless, talking about yourself with a therapist – actually with anyone — is a pure leap of faith. You have to step over that internal barrier that says "don't talk about what's really going on," slowly and at your own pace. When you feel pushed too far, say so. Respect your fear and resistance. Learn to acknowledge your perception of what seems okay or not okay. At the same time, be willing to take some risks and hang in there for yourself the way Sue Ann did. Gradually it works.

A CLIENT'S SURPRISE ABOUT HER OWN THOUGHTS

Many times clients say:

"Maybe I should be telling you what I'm thinking."

"I filter what I say to you."

"Sometimes I have thoughts I don't want to tell you about."

"I suppose you have to know what I'm thinking if you're going to be able to help me."

In sharing awareness of how much she held back from me, Nicole saw how little she shared of herself with anyone. She sighed, "I want to learn to reach out and get out of my isolation ward."

We identified important relationships to analyze the extent of her holding back and started with the man she was dating. Using role play, where she spoke for both herself and her friend, Jim, she revealed the nature of the relationship. He was open, questioning, sharing with her. She shut down with simple, one line responses. She said: "there's a wall in my head. I can't get around it." She paused, looked surprised, and said: "it's like talking to my mother!"

Now we focused on mom. When she was 13, Nicole returned from a party where there were kissing games. Excited about new and somewhat thrilling feelings, she shared the details of her evening and her attractions to boys. Her mother was furious. Instead of helping and guiding Nicole, she punished her. The result: she stopped talking about what she felt. First to her mother, then to her friends. It had become habitual, her way of being in the world and in relationships. The complexity of her fear kept her distant from others; more importantly, it kept her distant from what she felt and knew about herself.

As she began to open herself to her thoughts and feelings and share them in therapy, her relationships began to change. She risked knowing what was inside her and then risked intimacy in her relationships.

STOPPING IT FOR YOURSELF

Ask yourself: "What if I look inside and there is nothing there or I hate what I find?"

-Write as many thoughts as you can quickly.

-Don't edit; Be honest.

-Put down whatever comes into your mind.

-Review your answers and reflect on your physical and emotional reactions.

MAKE THE QUESTION LESS ANXIETY PROVOKING – REFRAME IT!

Diffuse your anxiety about the real you by writing your answers to a different question: "What am I afraid to feel, think, remember?"

-Write all the answers that come into your mind. Write until you get a true sense there is nothing else.

-Be honest with yourself. Don't edit.

-Check your physical and emotional state. Each time you go through this process you learn more about the negative power of your answers.

-Compare your answers to those from the negative questions: "What if I look inside and nothing is there or I hate what I find?" Write down anything you want to remember.

PAYING ATTENTION IS A MAJOR INGREDIENT IN THE RECEIPE FOR CHANGE

Both Sue Ann and Nicole learned to pay attention to themselves at a deep enough level to create change. But how did paying attention become a challenge? You are surrounded by demands; sometimes overwhelmed by the wants and needs of all the people in your life. A focus on *you* has to be a priority. Making yourself a priority, let alone putting yourself first more often, is counter to the messages you've received about maintaining relationships. The expectation is: *put others first*. If you feel that is a strong message or belief, it will be harder to shift gears. Deciding to examine who you are – in your important relationships, and in the systems you live and work in – either in therapy or in some form of self study, is a big step in the direction of *you* as a priority.

Paying attention is about waking up to the realities of your life. Naturally the answers to the questions you ask yourself, even when reframed in a productive manner, are sometimes depressing or anxiety ridden; however, they are the truth. Even when the truth is hard to handle, it is easier to tackle than all the past negative messages. Reflect on these thoughts when the negative questions persist:

> "I haven't spent enough time learning about me. It will make me anxious to start, but I need to feel my feelings even when they scare me. I can do that with help."

> "Facing thoughts and feelings about myself and my relationships is hard work. I am capable of hard work."

> "Taking a deeper look inside means changing the way I do things. I can honor that change is scary and still try to take some small manageable steps in the direction I want to go."

> "I don't have to do everything at once, I just have to act. I have to get started."

> "I deserve to know myself so I can make the best decisions for me. It's okay to be afraid as long as I don't let the fear paralyze me. I need some support to get started, and that's okay."

> "I know there are things about me that are good, positive. I will look at what I am doing right so I feel strong enough to look at the things that are so hard."

JANE'S DISCOVERIES

The true richness that can come from knowing yourself doesn't feel possible at the beginning. There is too much tension and self-doubt about what is really inside you. Consequently you can sometimes learn more through looking at the "end" of the process. What happens when you spend time in self-examination? What are you like when you have "completed" therapy? Jane's experience gives you some answers.

Jane grew up in a family with loving parents, but her mother had battled cancer for many years and died when Jane was 12. "I had to grow up fast," Jane said. "I had to help with Mom, and I felt responsible for my dad and my kid sister. They all needed me." As a result she moved into adulthood as the substitute mother, negating her own needs because there was no time or energy to discover them.

She described herself: " Everyone loves me, is nice to me, and I don't get it. I don't deserve it. I'm not who they think I am."

THE IMPACT OF THE FEAR

Jane had low self-esteem and a fear of failure that kept her from trying anything for herself. Mostly she feared looking inside and exploring her real feelings. "I always play it safe. Then I feel unhappy or bored or disappointed with my decisions." Her brief career in nursing was not satisfying, but she lamented, "I have no idea what I want instead. It's like my relationships. They end painfully because I don't know what kind of person I'm looking for."

RISKING CHANGE

In her 30's, Jane took her biggest risk. She began therapy. Her fear slowed the process, but she committed to taking care of herself and finding out who she was. She wanted to be in charge of her life. After one year of individual therapy and four years of group, Jane summarized her experience: "I've learned to know, love and trust the insides I was terrified to look at. I'm still struggling with a difficult relationship and an impending career change but I have the tools to handle those day to day realities and live my life for me."

She told the members of her group goodbye with sadness and affection, and great good humor. Here are some more of the things she shared: "I wouldn't have believed I could like myself, even if you had told me. In fact you probably did tell me! But when I think back on how scared I was, how hesitant I was to risk knowing myself.....I just wish there was a video tape for comparison!"

I know I am ready to leave. I have a kind of confidence I couldn't imagine was possible. I know I will always face problems, but I know how to take care of myself. I'm filled with good feelings and strength. I have great psychological muscle!"

WHAT'S NEXT?

If you are good at paying attention to others, you can also become good at paying attention to yourself. The energy you direct outward can make a U-turn and come back to you. As you experiment with this new focus, in the beginning, it won't feel right. You might even experience physical discomfort.

Remember you can congratulate yourself on becoming conscious of what's going on even if you don't like it. Consciousness is a giant step toward well-being. It allows you to make choices about your behavior, the actions that will make change possible. You will discover that behaving in a healthy and productive manner, will eventually alter the way you feel.

As you allow yourself to learn about who you really are, you will gradually like yourself more, and feel more confident. When you do encounter things in yourself you don't like, you won't be as scared. If you take your time and start exploring and embracing who you are, you will open the door to a truly new way of living your life.

CHAPTER SIX

QUESTION SIX: WHY DO I FEEL LIKE SUCH A CHILD? SO INCOMPETENT?

When people get angry with me and raise their voices, I don't exactly tilt my head to the side, twist my hair with my finger, and tell them what a nice girl I am, but sometimes I feel like doing it !   In a heartbeat I can become a child again, scared by anger, and thinking: "What can I do to defend myself?"

IT HAPPENS EVERY DAY OF YOUR LIFE!

Everyone feels like a child sometimes. Childish or child like behavior is frequently the reason conversations break down. Individual consciousness – identifying personal behavior or understanding what's going on in the behavior of others is limited but needed. How often do you think or say or hear someone else say:

"You're acting like a big baby!"

"We were discussing something important and all of a sudden I felt like I was talking to a six year old."

 "I don't know what happened to me, I just felt so little."

"My experience with my husband/partner last night made me feel like I live with a teenager."

 "I was doing a great job at _____ and suddenly I was acting like a kid."

"I need to get a grip! I sound like a child!"

YOU'RE SMARTER THAN YOU THOUGHT

When you intuitively know you are feeling or acting like a child or when you have that same thought about the person you are talking to – you're describing regression. The adult part of you or the adult part of the other person seems to have temporarily "disappeared."

BECOMING CHILDISH

Everyone regresses. That means you can "quickly get little." The negative form of regressing or "becoming little" happens when you are overly stressed – feeling scared, angry, or ashamed. Suddenly you truly feel and sound, and perhaps behave, as if you are two or four or fifteen! When that happens, the accompanying feelings are usually quite negative. The conversation goes off track or fails. The decisions needed are delayed or misdirected. So what is going on here?

JANET'S REGRESSION

Regressive energy pulls you back to a "child ego state." You are reacting to a current situation just as you reacted to something or someone similar when you were a child. It can feel like tumbling down the rabbit hole in the story of Alice In Wonderland! But for practical understanding, it's like falling into the full trash compacter described earlier. Here is a common example:

> Janet reported a conversation with her friend Ann that escalated into a disagreement. Ann is comfortable with conflict and easily supports her position. Janet becomes anxious when anyone disagrees with her or expresses anger. As a child she regularly felt the disapproval and anger of her parents. She survived the fear and anxiety she encountered with them by emotionally shutting down. As an adult she is still afraid of almost any conflict. It perplexes her and she laments, "I just can't get hold of myself."
>
> When her talk with Ann intensified, she reported, "I felt physically little, like I was listening to one of my parents. I couldn't think of a thing to say or do, I just wanted the conversation to end. I was so confused about my feelings I was dizzy. I guess I just gave up again. I'm so angry with myself for 'being such a child.'"

Janet doesn't understand why this happens to her so often. And Ann is bewildered that her friend, who is usually so easy to talk to, acts so withdrawn and inarticulate.

WHAT'S ACTUALLY HAPPENING HERE?

In this example, Janet's childhood history "takes over." She has not learned what "triggers" her reactions or what she might do to understand and change her behavior.

She is still surprised by the intensity of her feelings, and angry with herself that she grew so withdrawn. Hours later, she is perfectly capable of thinking through what she wanted to say. She also knows she wants to avoid doing anything to correct the miss-communication and can delay talking to her friend for several days. She does not understand what makes her incapable of thinking clearly and logically during a confrontation! She almost doesn't recognize herself. You can see how she might begin to wonder if there is "something wrong with her."

WHAT'S SO NEGATIVE ABOUT THIS QUESTION?

When you ask: "Why do I feel like such a child? So incompetent?" you may be able to hear the negative assumptions underneath the question. "I am a child and I shouldn't be!" "I can't take care of myself!" "There is something terribly wrong with me."

This kind of thinking produces even more childlike and helpless feelings. You reach a dead end, believing you can't do anything! And when you stay stuck in a six year old or ten year old emotional state, the dead end is logical. The capacity for problem solving, tackling a difficult situation and understanding what to do next is limited by the age of your regressive state. If you are feeling and thinking like a six year old, you can't think clearly about the problems you have at 40! If you were taught to be a responsible child, your six year old energy will try hard to solve the problem and become more scared that she can't do what she is supposed to do. If you were irresponsible at age six, you will probably run away – still frightened because you don't know what to do.

Sorting through regression alters your ability, over time, to problem solve effectively.

Ask yourself the question again: "Why do I feel like such a child? So incompetent?"

-Write your answers. Write everything that comes to you.

-Remember to be honest with yourself. Don't edit.

-Review your answers and reflect on your physical and emotional reactions.

A SMALL CHANGE MAKES A BIG DIFFERENCE

The change in the unhealthy question, "Why do I feel like such a child?" is slight but important: "<u>What or who</u> makes me feel like a child?"

-Answer this question by writing down absolutely anything that comes to you. Keep writing until you know you have nothing else to say.

 -Be honest with yourself. Don't edit.

-Reflect on your physical and emotional responses.

-Compare your responses to your answers to the negative question.

-Write whatever you are aware of.

EXPLORING REGRESSION FOR DEEPER UNDERSTANDING

Getting little when you don't want to causes problems in every area of your life. When you regress in situations where you are invested in firm, clear, and decisive communication – an important meeting at work or a difficult confrontation with a family member – it feels even more confusing. Many women report crying when they need to be firm and strong in a business setting. Others report backing away from asking for something they want and need from a spouse, family member or friend. Because it happens frequently, see if you can understand your own regressive behavior with some additional questions:

-When you feel little or unable to function appropriately, where are you? Describe in detail all the situations that come to mind. Let yourself travel as far back in time as you can.

-When you feel little or unable to function appropriately, who are the people you are interacting with? List the names. Don't leave anyone out!

-When you feel little in your conversations with _____, who does she/he remind you of? Pick one name at a time from the last question to fill in this blank. You can answer this question with everyone from your previous list.

-When was the last time you felt little? Specifically, how old did you feel? Try to write down the very first age that pops into your mind. If you are tempted to discount the first thought, trust yourself! Write the age. Now write about your life when you were that age. With no attention to form or structure, describe as much as you can about this time in your life, what was going on, and how you felt.

USING YOUR ANSWERS

Your answers may clear up some puzzling experiences you've had with important people in your life. Look for patterns. Identify the names and situations that continue to appear in your answers. Take some time and make journal entries when you get insights you don't want to lose.

Also see if the responses of other women help you build perspective.

HOW DO OTHER WOMEN RESPOND TO THE NEGATIVE FORM OF THE QUESTION?

" I guess I can't grow up. I was two years old the minute she raised her voice."

"I let him treat me just like my dad. I will always live like this little girl."

"I was a tearful baby in the meeting. No wonder no one trusts me. I can't trust myself – anywhere."

"I'm so ashamed of my childish behavior with my husband/partner. I can't face him/her. And I don't know what makes me do it."

"I feel pretty crazy and off center when I act so childish… and it concerns me."

"When the chips are down and I feel like I'm 10, I get frightened. I couldn't even keep it together in a silly little argument, for god's sake!"

"Just when I think this therapy is working, I blow it again with childish behavior."

"I hate myself when I act like such a childish, spoiled brat. I don't know why she/he wants a relationship with me. I wouldn't want one."

"I couldn't think, I couldn't feel, I couldn't talk. I might as well have been sucking my thumb and pulling my ear!

"I started the conversation in a strong and firm voice and ended up in tears. I couldn't stop myself."

"I think I know what I need to do, but a "stubborn little girl" in me stops me. I actually feel my heels dig in."

"Too often I don't feel like a grown up."

"I'm scared of how powerful this child in me is."

DO SO MANY WOMEN FEEL SO CHILDLIKE?

 Many women think of themselves in childlike terms. When that is the healthy, playful, creative child, that's just fine. It's creative and fun. But much of the time, regression is about pain and anger that needs recognition and healing. When you berate yourself about acting childish, consider these answers.

"These old feelings aren't bad or crazy, they just don't get the results I want and deserve."

"There is a pattern in my behavior. Every time I talk to _____ or someone who reminds me of _____ I feel and act like I'm about _____. Seeing that will help me change, but it hurts like hell to see it and feel it."

"I've always had some degree of trouble with authority figures/men/women/ _____, and I have felt stuck and made decisions that weren't good for me. Maybe I can change this!"

"I'm not a child, I just feel that way sometimes. I'm afraid to face this reality, but it's okay to be afraid. I don't have to do it all by myself."

"I get little when I'm scared or angry or in pain. This behavior doesn't mean I'm crazy. I can do something about it even if it does take time."

RECOGNITION IS THE BEGINNING OF CHANGE

These answers speak of recognition and insight, and acknowledge that awareness means hard work. Looking at and understanding your childish thoughts, feelings and behaviors, then using what you learn can help you make necessary changes.

AN IMAGE TO REMEMBER

Imagine you have a vanity mirror in your hand. One side produces a fairly accurate image of you, the adult. The flip side of this mirror is a magnifier. It makes you look much bigger and distorts your perception. You might not even recognize yourself until you look carefully. Falling back into the feelings of your childhood is like suddenly looking at the magnified image of you. It's bigger than the adult reflection, potent, and initially unrecognizable. Your adult has disappeared. This out-sized childish image takes over and distorts your reality, making you feel helpless and incompetent. When you see more clearly, you can understand, one step at a time, even if you are scared.

A PARADOX

Your system is actually trying to help when it "drags" you into the contents of the trash compactor. You are periodically pulled back to feeling states in childhood, adolescence, young adulthood. You revisit those situations and experiences to clearly understand the patterns that have unfolded in your life. Patterns develop as a result of the things you learned growing up. Exploring those patterns helps you celebrate the good things you learned and aids you in identifying the things you learned that keep getting in your way.

WAS IT A BAD DECISION?

Your choices and decisions as a child, your beliefs and conclusions about life formed your way of understanding and coping with your universe. You did the only thing you could at the time.

But the decisions you made as a child in response to fear, anger, pain and shame are generally not useful to you as an adult. They helped you survive and feel safe then, but they probably have the opposite effect on your feelings and behavior now.

JACKIE'S DISCOVERY

Jackie had recently made some changes in her life as a result of therapy. She had started spending Wednesday evenings with a group of her women friends. Her partner was supportive, understanding Jackie needed her own separate time. But one Wednesday night Jackie came home from her girlfriend evening almost two hours late. When she came in the door, Melissa was waiting for her: "Where the hell have you been? I was worried sick! Why didn't you call me?"

Jackie had arrived feeling guilty for not paying attention to the time, ready to apologize. But Melissa's words sent a rage flowing through her. She flinched and backed away, stomping around the house, yelling, "You want to control my whole life. I won't have it. You're a royal bitch! I'll just live by myself." She ended up sleeping in their guest bedroom and was immediately remorseful. She spent a restless, guilt-filled night, but stayed put, feeling too stubborn to go apologize, and a little scared by the severity of her reaction.

RESOLUTION AND THE BEGINNING OF CHANGE

The next day, Jackie apologized the minute she got up. They had built a strong relationship that worked most of the time, and they managed to resolve the conflict by talking through their respective feelings. But Jackie was puzzled by her intense reactions. I asked her to picture herself back in the fight with Melissa. "How old were you?" I asked.

Her jaw dropped. "I was 16!" Instantly she pictured her angry encounters with her father when she had first begun to date, often risking coming in after curfew.

"I'm still fighting with my dad, not Melissa. Her anger was fairly legitimate. Mine was just like it was when I was 16. No wonder I felt confused."

USING THE PRESENT TO UNRAVEL THE PAST

This knowledge helped her separate old, historical anger from current anger, making it much easier to express her feelings firmly and directly rather than yelling inappropriately.

When an encounter today is similar in energy and content to unresolved historical conflicts, the old and the new merge with palpable forcefulness. It can happen quickly, defeating your ability to "think about what you want to do or say." Some clients describe having no control over words and actions. Some say they are momentarily not themselves.

Many life decisions and actions, like Jackie's, have been, and still are, based on the beliefs and decisions made in childhood! Many early decisions work just fine when they have been refined and developed over the years. You want to change those that get in your way, the ones that are automatic and unexamined and interfere with your conscious thinking and decision making.

IT'S HARD WORK

Even healthy questions can dig up unresolved fear and shame. Reframed questions lead you into the historic contents of the trash compactor in a way that works.

You know by now that many of the questions you have been reading and answering are hard. They ask you to face the difficult and painful parts of your life. And at the same time, they show you a way forward, allowing you to change course in a healthy, happy direction. If you are struggling to understand what to do to feel better, or if you begin to be afraid or anxious, don't try to answer these questions alone. And always, always talk to someone when you are afraid of what you think and feel.

CHAPTER SEVEN

QUESTION SEVEN: WHY CAN'T I HAVE A GOOD RELATIONSHIP? WHY DO I KEEP FAILING?

From the time I first walked, I carried a baby doll in a pink blanket, feeding, burping, changing it – learning to make a relationship my focus. You, too, were probably taught by family, schools and churches – society in general – to make relationships your focus.

WHAT DO YOU BELIEVE ABOUT RELATIONSHIPS? MARRIAGE? AND FAMILY?

With few exceptions, most girls grow up believing they will get married or at least have a primary, permanent relationship with someone they love. In addition, most assume they will have children, and create a family. Although the definition of family may change, even expand, as you grow up, the responsibility for connectedness, relating and being a part of a larger whole forms a value base for most women. Many women automatically assume "This is what I'll do, this is who I'll be."

GROWING UP FEMALE

Forming and maintaining relationships is a "role assignment" you receive early in life. You learn to view the world and yourself through the relationships you establish. This "assignment," creates a yardstick you use to measure, judge, and evaluate your progress.

When you make a decision that varies from the original "assignment," the old yardstick appears for a "measurement check." Consequently, if you haven't done it the way you were "expected to do it," you can easily judge yourself as a failure. Certainly you can start to question yourself – asking "What's wrong with me, anyway?"

BEHIND IN MY DEVELOPMENTAL TASKS!

I almost always felt out of step with the yardstick I was taught to use. I was single when everyone was getting married; building a career when friends were having babies; marrying when others were divorcing; being a step-parent to young children when my friends were seeing kids off to college; divorcing when peers and friends and colleagues were finally getting new relationships underway; living with someone when it was finally back in vogue to marry again; and never giving birth!

Humor helped me mask the pain when I was judged by others as "out of step." I thought I had accepted that I was different, but I discovered I was kidding myself. No matter how good I felt about my choices, I felt others measured me as a failure. My mother certainly did! The biggest shock was my recognition of what I did to myself. In a secret corner of my mind, when I was younger, I called myself a failure!

GET A NEW YARDSTICK!

The yardstick that measures success or failure is deeply ingrained in most women. Because it's an old, outdated measuring device, you're hard on yourself when relationships aren't successful. You have a great deal riding on the successful relationship outcome; it's the way you are evaluated as a woman completing her "assignment."

In this context, the questions, "Why can't I have a good relationship?" or "Why do I keep failing?" are vital. Your answers might be something like this: "I still haven't figured out what is wrong with me and why I keep screwing up every good relationship." Or, "I mess up every relationship I'm in because I am just bad at relating." The root belief in either response is the same: "It's me! I'm a mess! I wouldn't want to have a relationship with me either! I keep making the same mistakes."

CHECK YOUR OWN ANSWERS

Ask yourself again: "Why can't I have a good relationship? Why do I keep failing?"

-Write all your answers as they pop into your mind.

-Remember. Don't edit, and be honest with yourself.

-Reflect on what you feel physically and emotionally.

-Write anything you are aware of.

COMPARE YOURSELF TO OTHER WOMEN

Answers to this question are usually about seeing yourself as a failure and about unending blame, guilt and recrimination. Relationships fill our thoughts as well as our lives; and reading the thoughts of other women builds perspective.

"I've ruined more relationships than ten people put together."

"I don't know what's wrong with me. I am so self destructive when it comes to intimacy. I always do the wrong thing."

"I heard myself and I couldn't stop talking, ruining everything! "

"Women/men never stay with me after the first few weeks. They find out what I'm like quickly."

"I've been married and divorced two times. I'm embarrassed to fail again but I know I can't make this marriage work."

"I'm in my third relationship with an alcoholic. I thought I found someone different this time, but I keep making the same dumb choices. Why can't I get it right just once?"

"I'm going to age and die alone. I can't stand it. I don't know what I keep doing wrong."

"I think I'm just too difficult to live with."

"My spouse/partner/significant other says I'm just too sensitive. I guess that must be the problem I can't fix."

"I know I'm a pain in the ass – even my mother says so."

"I have friends, but I always have trouble keeping them. Maybe people just don't like me after they get to know me."

"My kids are behaving the way I did as a child. I'm making them as insecure and bad at relating as I am!"

"The relationship just isn't as important to my spouse/partner as it is to me. I'm so insecure and needy that I end up driving men/women away."

"They can tell immediately that all I want is to get married and have kids.

I must have it written on my forehead. I think I'm stupid to have no other goals."

"I end up fighting all the time – even when there's nothing really wrong. It feels pretty crazy inside me."

"I know what I need to do to make the conversation turn in the right direction, but a part of me refuses to give in and do it. I end up damaging the relationship."

"I'm so depressed when my relationships go bad. I don't ever want another one, but I'm afraid I can't function without one."

"My kids hate me. I yell at them all the time. I hate myself, too. I'm worse than my mother or father ever hoped to be."

"I'm terrified to be in a relationship – I'm terrified to be alone. God, there is no place that feels good to me."

"I've been confused about my sexuality all my life. I've been married for years, and I know there's something wrong with me because I can't make myself want to be here with this man."

"I've never had a relationship with a person who's available. They are married or living with someone else. I know there's something wrong with this picture – and it's me."

"I've screwed up my life by putting my career first. I've ruined relationships because I can't give them quality time. Now there's just a big void in my life."

WELL, MAYBE THERE'S SOME TRUTH IN WHAT WOMEN SAY ABOUT THIS!

Women have a lot to say about relationships! Unfortunately, the negative feelings are generally about you, not about the relationship. These laments highlight one major truth: relationships are important to most women. They appear essential to our core of well being.

You do not have to feel bad about yourself because you make relationships a priority; building and nurturing relationships is one of your admirable strengths. You do, however, need to understand your behavior if it isn't getting you what you want, or if you are out of balance.

IT WILL BE HARD TO STOP QUESTIONING YOURSELF ABOUT RELATIONSHIPS!

Negative questions are hard to shake. This is especially true when the subject is key relationships. Reflect on some of these answers when the negative form of the question stays "stuck" in your head.

> "Relationships are important to me and that's okay; however, my behavior is getting in the way of having the kind of relationship I want. I can examine my behavior and make changes even when it's painful."

> "I must repeat mistakes for a reason. I can analyze my patterned behaviors so I don't continue to get in my own way. And I will stop and change the sentence when I call myself stupid!"

> "The men/women I struggle with appear similar. Examining the traits and behaviors they share will help me understand my responses."

> "My behavior with my kids scares me. But I am not my mother or my father. I learned some things when I was growing up I need help to stop."

> "I am not in this relationship by myself. He/she is contributing to the problem, and I can examine that, too."

> "I truly dislike some of my behaviors but I'm not bad or crazy."

> "It's okay that I value my relationships, but I make them too important, and shifting even a little may help me."

> "I don't want to be alone all my life, but if I am I can learn to have meaning and be fully alive."

> "I want to learn that I am loveable. I'm going to need help because I feel a big barrier in me to that belief."

> "I expect too much of my primary relationships and I put too much pressure on them.

> "Being true to my sexuality feels healthy even if the pressure to somehow

change is strong. There is nothing sick or bad about my sexual preference."

"The decisions I have made recently have created pain and unhappiness. I can learn to handle my reality and change when I am ready. It is time for me to look myself squarely in the eye."

TAKE YOUR RELATIONSHIP "TEMPERATURE"

What's the truth about you and the relationships in your life? Take a few minutes and find out with the nine questions below.

First, reframe the original question so that you direct your attention to your actual behavior. "What happened in my relationship with _____ that kept it from being successful?"

Write your answers and complete the process suggested in each chapter for reflecting and comparing your responses.

Now continue "taking your temperature." Take your time. Answer the questions at your own pace. Skip questions and return to them later if you need to. Use the workbook/journal appendix if you need more space to write.

ONE. What behaviors do you engage in that have a negative impact on your relationships? Make separate lists for each relationship, both at home and at work.

TWO. In your relationship with _____, what does she/he do that you don't like?

THREE: What is your relationship with _____ like? When you picture the two of you together, what words best describe the relationship?

FOUR: When you begin a new relationship, what are your expectations? Of yourself? Of the other person?

FIVE: When you begin a new relationship, what do you want the other person to know about you? How do you provide that information? When? Compare a romantic relationship to a work relationship.

SIX: Reflect on one or two important relationships. What are your resentments? Your regrets? Your appreciations? Make separate lists for each relationship and each category.

SEVEN: List your most important relationships – spouses, partners, people you have dated, your children, close friends, anyone you have lived with or related to for a long time. Under each name write the negative and positive characteristics of the individual. If your parents or primary caretakers were not on your list, identify their negative and positive characteristics. Review your lists. Compare the similarities between your parents or caretakers and your relationships with the other important people in your life.

EIGHT: Reflect on one or more relationships in any area of your life you feel good about. List the things you do well in the relationship. Did you do any of these things in the relationships that ended badly?

NINE: Review your thoughts and write your definition of a good relationship. Separate your personal and work definitions.

AND YOUR TEMPERATURE IS?

Hopefully, you feel just a little better about yourself as a result of this reflection. The questions help you focus on positives as well as negatives, and they help you tell yourself the truth. Even when the truth turns out to be negative and painful, you now have a more realistic look at yourself and your problems in relationships. With detailed attention to the questions, you can see specific behaviors and unfolding patterns. With this concrete information, you can direct your energy toward problem solving and change. If this seems like a great deal of work, it is!

BEVERLY WANTED TO DIE RATHER THAN FAIL

> Beverly's old patterns in relationships had created so much pain that she was suicidal when she began therapy. She thought she either had to divorce her third husband or kill herself. "I know I'm making the same mistakes over and over. I see the pattern and I feel crazy and self-destructive. Sometimes I even think I am afraid to succeed! I would rather die than live like this another day."

> We began by looking at the similarities in her three husbands who were all emotionally unavailable workaholics, focused on career and success at

all costs. At first she saw no similarity to her parents; she believed she had done an excellent job in choosing men totally different from her alcoholic father.

But gradually, Beverly began to talk about how she grew up: "My father was always drinking, kind of tranced out. I couldn't talk to him about anything important...there was no one *in there*."

She hadn't thought about the imprint of her mom, assuming that her choices of men were solely related to her dad. She admitted, "It's hard to accept how much my husbands have in common with my mother. But I see it – hard working, determined, gone all the time, and emotionally unavailable. Wow!"

SEEING THE PATTERNS HELPS

Beverly kept choosing men who shared characteristics with both her parents. She was drawn, as we all are, to familiarity. As a child, she withdrew from her parents and their lack of attention, to protect herself from further hurt. She left the family at the first possible opportunity. Beverly realized she did the same thing in her first two marriages – she left to protect herself from any more pain. She was about to repeat the behavior a third time.

This time, she experimented with changing her own behavior. As she dealt with old pain in therapy, she was courageous enough to move toward her husband, rather than away from him. Gradually, she let go of trying to change him. As she focused on ways to connect rather than distance, she was shocked: "I'm so afraid of intimacy – the very thing I want so badly!" Over time, her husband responded and came to therapy. Together they are exploring their individual and relationship patterns and changing them. Each time they make their old behaviors conscious, they get a little closer. They still have a lot of work to do, but they finally trust their ability to do it!

MY PATTERNS WERE TOUGH FOR ME TO SEE

Understanding patterns can be extremely helpful, but they aren't always easy to uncover. My own patterns, through a series of bad relationships, were quite illusive to me.

After years of reflection, I believed I always picked men like my dad because I loved him so much – even though he was emotionally unavailable to me – and that I just had trouble "unhooking" myself from that well ingrained behavior. I berated myself for continuing to make such bad choices. I was drawn to men who were emotionally unavailable either as a result of "workaholism" or their difficulty with genuine intimacy.

CAN YOU AVOID INTIMACY AND NOT KNOW IT?

Gradually, I discovered I was focusing on the wrong issue. Yes, the men I picked were, indeed, emotionally unavailable. Yes, I was drawn to them because they were so much like my dad. But the deepest problem was my own avoidance of intimacy. This was not easy for me to examine. I unconsciously picked men who didn't want a connection so I could protect myself from loving someone who might hurt me – again. Very similar to Beverly! I, however, had the added "advantage" of being able to blame the men for the failed relationships, taking myself off the hook. When I started looking at my family issues more carefully, I was able to break out of my destructive pattern.

GOING STIR CRAZY FROM MIXED MESSAGES

The countless double messages you hear about relating effectively and, at the same time, being your own person, add to the confusion.

-You have to be in a relationship to be a real woman.

-You are too dependent on relationships.

-Put your relationships first.

-Remember to take care of yourself.

-Make being a wife/partner and mother your priority.

-Make being a career woman/having a good job a priority so you can take care of yourself.

-Be dependent.

-Be independent.

MAKE YOUR OWN LIST

You can probably generate your own list. Whatever the dichotomies are, it is important to bring them into consciousness. When you are aware of your internal messages, they are less likely "to trip you up" or throw you off balance.

Mixed messages create internal conflict and force either-or thinking. They cause you to be critical of yourself; whatever it is you are doing, there is always something else you should be doing instead. So women swing back and forth, criticizing themselves endlessly.

BALANCE! BALANCE! BALANCE!

Clients and workshop participants tell me the advice to balance their personal and work lives is next to impossible. The "balance is necessary" message feels similar to the "superwoman syndrome" from the 1980's when women were told to do everything and do it well.

"Integration" has a more gentle message. The integration of your individuality with your intimacy is key for a comfortable life. Valuing relationships is an essential aspect of being a woman. You will find some who criticize you for this, saying it defeats your effectiveness in the world of work. Your focus on relating and interacting, on nurturing and caring brings wholeness to you and to those you relate to; but only when you integrate your own unique needs as an individual.

A CHANGE IN PERSPECTIVE

Your "homework" is to discover and heal the negatives you carry around about relating. When you are unhappy about your relationships you are probably taking far too much responsibility for the success or failure of the relationship. Perhaps you are working too hard on the wrong things – evaluating yourself with external standards (that outdated yardstick), repeating old patterns, and keeping yourself off center.

The change process starts with your own definition of a healthy relationship. Take a hard look at the family you grew up in, where you developed your earliest ideas about relationships and intimacy.

BUT I SWORE I WOULD BE DIFFERENT

Though you may have vowed to make your marriage or partnership different from that of your parents or primary caretakers, you carry the powerful imprint of their beliefs and behaviors. Continue to work with the healthy questions and explore the behaviors that get in your way.

FINALLY, A STARTING POINT FOR BEING DIFFERENT

Think about the relationships you find challenging. List them by name and then pick one to examine in depth. Describe the relationship – the behavior of the person – your behavior.

What is it in your behavior that makes the relationship challenging? Assume the other person will continue to behave the way she/he always does. Look at your behaviors and list them: "I don't listen." "I become defensive." "I get scared and shut down." "I am quick to anger."

Pick one aspect of your behavior you truly believe you are ready to change. Get started. Write it down.

One relationship behavior I am ready to change is _____

Identify someone you could practice with: a friend, a colleague, a family member, a minister. Tell the individual what you are working on and ask for help.

If you think you are ready to work on the specific relationship you want to improve, tell the individual what behavior you want to change. "I need to improve my ability to listen, so I am going to take more time to make sure I really hear everything you are saying to me. Sometimes I may ask you to repeat what you said or I will try to paraphrase what you said. I want to make sure you understand what I'm trying to do and that you are okay with it."

Whatever you choose, go at your own pace and be prepared for making mistakes and slipping back into old ways of behaving. Have faith in your ability to live life more fully. You deserve to have the relationships that are healthy and fun.

CHAPTER EIGHT

QUESTION EIGHT: WHY CAN'T I COUNT ON ANYONE?

Women are experts at masking the discontent and disappointment they feel in relation to others! "Why can't I count on anyone?" "Why can't I trust anyone?" "When is it my turn?" "Does anyone anywhere see me or understand me?" "Do I just expect too much or is there something really wrong with me?"

You ask these potent questions when you lay awake at 3:00 a.m., worrying over problems and feeling you have no one to turn to. Experiment with asking the questions out loud, then writing them down. Hearing and seeing the negative question can help diminish the intensity.

HOW CAN YOU FEEL ALONE WHEN YOU'RE ALWAYS WORKING AT RELATING?

It may seem illogical that women feel so alone and misunderstood considering how hard we work at making connections. But many of you feel you don't receive as much as you give. Many of you report getting almost nothing in return for the hours of energy and attention you direct to others. You sometimes feel a palpable yearning, a dissatisfaction – perhaps even a lack of safety – and you usually can't quite describe it, can't quite put a label on what you feel . You just know you are missing something that is important to you.

WHAT IS IT I NEED, ANYWAY?

Sometimes you can't quite describe what you are after in life because you have never had it! You have adapted so well to your life "as is" that you don't see what isn't there. Yet you are stuck with a vague sense of needing – sometimes yearning for something you can't quite define.

One question to ask is "How would it feel to receive some of the caring and nurturing I give to others?" Many of you stay stuck, feeling disappointed, hesitant, and afraid to expect good things, to ask for what you want even when you can define what that is.

But don't forget to explore the possibility that you don't give anything, or enough, to others. If you have spent a huge chunk of your life over functioning in your relationships – extending yourself to others and neglecting your own needs – you may have reached a point of withdrawing from intimate connections or feeling angry and resentful of the people to whom you want to feel love and connection.

TERESA'S STORY

Teresa came to therapy while in the middle of a third divorce. She was leaving her husband because nothing was working the way she wanted. She was sad, scared, and extremely angry. "I can't figure out what is wrong with me, but I keep having this cold empty feeling – like never being filled up. No, like always being hungry! No, like being hungry and having no idea what would be satisfying to eat!"

After several sessions of gently probing, she finally talked about her childhood, the earliest pieces of the puzzle. Both her parents worked. They were good, caring people. They were stressed and physically exhausted. They put all their energy into saving money to educate their four children. As Teresa remembered her early years, she defended their hard work, "I benefited from every hour they put in!

DESCRIBING VS BLAMING

This exclamation created another minor road block. Teresa felt she was blaming them, a common feeling among clients when they begin to talk about challenging family history. I carefully explained the importance of describing events and behaviors in whatever detail possible. Blaming fccls so cnergetically angry, defensive, and uncomfortable, the difference gradually begins to feel more clear.

Emotionally and physically Teresa got little from her parents. They expressed their love by providing for her materially. After weeks of therapy she tearfully sighed, "I just needed some time and attention, someone to talk to, a hug once in a while." Her parents didn't have it to give. At first it was hard for Teresa to express this loss. Initially it was just a physical sensation of emptiness. Holding her hand over her solar plexus, she would say, "It's like a big black hole right here."

MAKING IMPORTANT CONNECTIONS

"It's almost like I've been trying to fill the hole with men," she said. "I've been in so many unsatisfying relationships. I leave angry and more unhappy. I can't decide whether to blame them or me!"

After a year of therapy, Teresa saw two basic patterns that got in her way. First, she learned: "I'm drawn to people like my   parents. The men in my life have been good, caring people, but they expressed their love materially. They were never available, not physically affectionate, and never had the time to sit and talk, or to focus energy on me."

Second, she realized: "I have trouble taking care of myself, and understanding who I am and what I really want. I haven't been able to ask for it because I didn't know what 'it' was." Teresa only knew something was missing. When she understood what she wanted, she started taking better care of herself.

WHAT MADE IT HARD FOR TERESA?

Teresa grew up without a model of self-care. When you see adults take good care of themselves and you, it "registers." It "sticks" emotionally, behaviorally, and intellectually. Teresa's parents worked so hard providing physical security and well-being they neglected the intimate words and behaviors of good parenting. The complex connection to understand, is you are likely to "parent" yourself the way you were parented – things you did not receive growing up are often hard for you to give yourself as an adult.

When Teresa started taking care of herself, she began making better choices in all her relationships. She felt understood and connected with others because she was understanding and connecting with herself. Teresa worked long and hard at getting her life headed in the right direction. Each small improvement motivated her to keep at it.

TERESA'S THERAPY HOMEWORK

In therapy, Teresa spent a great deal of time reflecting and answering questions I gave her. Here are some of the questions she used to explore her feeling. If they seem relevant, use them.

-When you think about counting on, trusting someone, what do you feel?

What do you think? (If the difference doesn't seem clear, remember that feelings are one word like: scared, sad, angry, happy, joyful.)

What is your most disappointing experience with counting on or trusting someone? Describe it in detail. If writing about it brings other situations or people to mind, write about them, too.

-What decisions have you made or what conclusions have you arrived at regarding trusting others? Write down what sentences or words pop into your mind. An example might be, "I will never trust anyone. It's not safe."

-Identify one or two people you've counted on about something minor.

-Identify one or two people you've counted on about something deeply important to you.

-Think about the people you have identified. Describe the qualities or behaviors that allow you to regard them as safe to count on or trust.

-Think about your parents or primary caretakers. Were they people you trusted or counted on? If yes, what behaviors made them trustworthy. If no, what behaviors made them untrustworthy? List things they did or did not do to make you feel seen, heard, understood, loved.

-What makes you someone to count on or trust? What makes you someone who listens, understands, anticipates, nurtures? Make a list that describes your qualities and/or behavior. Where did you learn these things?

WHAT'S WRONG WITH ME

-What does it feel like to count on and trust yourself? What are the things you do for yourself that are loving, nurturing, and understanding?

-Think about the people you live with, work with, and socialize with. Write down the names of anyone you believe you can trust or count on. Be honest with yourself.

-What are you willing to change about your life to feel safer, more understood, heard, seen and loved and appreciated?

For example, consider telling one important person in your life you often feel disconnected and unappreciated. Or pick one person to ask for something you really want and need. And if both of these suggestions sound too hard, think of something you could do to reach out that produces the least amount of anxiety. The smallest effort will make a difference.

-What is the spiritual dimension of your life like? Do you feel open to a higher power? Do you have a sense of faith? Do you want to develop this part of your life more?

BACK TO THE ORIGINAL QUESTION

It's important to acknowledge your negative thoughts and feelings. Ask again,

"Why can't I count on anyone?"

-Write everything that comes into your mind. -Don't edit, and be honest with yourself.

-Reflect on what you feel physically and emotionally.

See if you are learning to observe the thoughts that pop up as well as the feelings and sensations in your body. Expand this reflection. Are you conscious of any spiritual issues?

-Write anything you are aware of.

THIS IS HARD. WHAT DO OTHER WOMEN HAVE TO SAY?

Most women are encouraged by the stories of others. They are relieved they aren't the "only one" to have ever thought such a thing. It's especially encouraging to see that someone is still "alive and well" after surviving such difficulties.

Here are more female voices:

"I knock myself out for my family and what happens if I ask for something? I'm invisible! I just quit asking, a long time ago."

"How will I know if I can trust you? Why should I? I don't trust anyone."

"Just once I would like for someone to pay attention to me the way I do them!"

"I can't trust men. I can't trust anyone. I can't even trust you."

"I exhaust myself being understanding. Sometimes I know what my husband/partner is going to say or ask for before he/she says it. How come I'm the only mind reader in this house?"

"I wonder what it would be like to have someone I love anticipate my needs. I hate asking for what I want. It's degrading. I can't get the words out of my mouth."

"Will it ever really be my turn."

"I don't have a clue about what I want. I just seem to know I don't like anything about what I have."

"I don't have the words for what I want. I just know I am lonely and sad. I feel separate even when people are around me. It feels really nutty because most women would kill for my life."

"My husband/partner/significant other is nice and attentive to everyone – solicitous even. It never happens with me. I guess I just don't deserve to be treated well. Nobody has ever treated me well, and I believed it would be different with him/her. I don't think it will ever be different."

"My mother/father never understood who I really am. I learned who they wanted me to be. Today they have no idea what my life is really like. They don't even care enough to ask me a question about what's important to me."

"If things were really bad, if I was in real honest to goodness trouble, I don't think I have anyone I could count on to understand and help. And I have lots of so-called friends."

"I would never hurt myself, but sometimes I think it would be okay to go to sleep and just not wake up."

EXPERIMENT WITH REFRAMING

These negative answers are sad, angry, and exhausted and filled with words like never, impossible, can't, always, nobody, everyone. It causes you to focus on defeats. Such answers cause you to feel powerless. Changing the question doesn't fix it, but it can get you pointed in a better direction.

Come up with your new version of the question. Always watch for even the slightest shift in your thought process, your feelings, and any sensations in your body. Then go through the same process of writing and reflecting.

If you aren't confident about reframing, ask this question instead or use it to compare to the one you've written. "When I have allowed myself to count on, trust someone, what happened?"

LEGITIMATE REASONS FOR THESE NEGATIVE QUESTIONS

Assuming many of your answers to the new question are still painful, you may see that you question the wisdom of counting on others. There are many reasons for your distrustful, questioning attitude.

THE PARENTING EXPLANATION

Many little girls grow up without enough of the loving attention they need. Instead, you are taught, at a young age, how to provide loving attention to others. Because you learned to anticipate the needs of others, you also logically expected that you, too, would be taken care of. Someone will pay attention to your needs and respond to you, just as you do to them. When your parents or primary caretakers don't provide enough of that attention, and your needs are not being met, you might feel:

"There is something terribly wrong with me."

Or, "It must be bad to ask for anything."

Or, "I guess I'm going to have to do it all by myself."

The feeling that something is wrong with you can slowly shift to anger and resentment, and then the thoughts and feelings might be:

"Why am I the only mind-reader in this **!!* family?"

Or, "I must be a really difficult person for people to figure out!"

Or, "Maybe nobody really cares enough to try."

Slowly, the progression of negative thinking pulls you back to a foundational assumption of negativity about yourself. "It's me. I'm the problem!"

THE LOGIC OF CHILDHOOD IS TRULY DIFFERENT

In childhood, it actually feels "safer" to see the problem as yours rather than conclude that your parents aren't doing a good job. As an adult, looking back, you are more able to see and understand your parents' weaknesses. But that same knowledge is terrifying to a child.

As a kid, if you decide you're the problem, you can hold on to hope. "If I'm just good enough, if I change, if I become a better girl, then things will be okay. They will love me and take care of me." The thoughts are a form of "self-soothing." Comforting thoughts, repeated regularly, become comforting beliefs.

As an adult, examine how that childhood belief has impacted you, especially if those conclusions translate into self-blame and the on-going assumptions that you are the problem.

WHAT YOU SEE IS WHAT YOU GET

My growing up provided confusing double messages. My parents paid a great deal of attention to basic needs, and they were physically present, providing or doing lots of wonderful things for me. But they were "emotionally absent" – unable to respond to my feelings. I did not get "emotional guidance," and at a young age I assumed I was expected to figure things out for myself, and naturally, do it right!

DO AS I SAY, NOT AS I DO.

The most confusing thing was what I saw. My mother sacrificed herself to everyone and everything. She did wonderful things for her parents, my father's parents, for me and my friends, for our small community. People adored her, and that served as reinforcement for doing more. But underneath, her own needs and desires went unmet. I sensed her anger and disappointment on a daily basis.

I DIDN'T SEE THE MOST IMPORTANT THING

Observing my mother gave me no model for asking for what I wanted or needed. She never counted on anyone, trusted anyone. The result? I inherited her mistrust, her assumptions that, "I will have to do this myself."

Learning to do it differently has been one of my biggest challenges. My doubt in the advisability of counting on others is a lingering thought that sometimes surges into consciousness. The difference is I can hear the thought, examine it, and make a more informed decision. Well engrained beliefs sometimes stay with you, but mindfulness helps you examine them before they head you in a negative, self-destructive direction.

A CULTURAL EXPLANATION

It is hard to digest the reality that women, as a group, aren't fully valued in our culture. Actually it is easier to deny it by pointing to the positive aspects of being female, of living in such a bountiful country. Those thoughts and beliefs are also important, but not looking at the total reality in our society is sometimes dangerous to your intellectual, emotional, physical and spiritual well being.

I can think of nothing about being female that is negative; however, it is necessary to see and confront the way females are defined and under- valued in our culture. When you thankfully see many individual women, perhaps even yourself, achieve success, acknowledgement, appreciation, it is more challenging to observe the group dynamic. Still it is essential to see the difference in how women as a group rather than as individuals, are defined and treated.

SECOND CLASS CITIZENS

When you live in a world that sees women as "second class citizens" it's hard for you not to internalize the message that you somehow aren't as deserving – of time, energy, and resources.

The message that you don't quite measure up, and are, therefore, undeserving, comes from the media, the church, the school, the corporation, and the community. Perhaps those messages alone are enough to get you to stop asking for anything for yourself. Or perhaps they were enough to keep you from learning anything about asking. Today, after all that brain washing, it can feel far too late to learn to count on people.

ARE YOU SAFE?

How does not feeling physically safe impact your trust levels? Is it something you consciously consider? My sense of my physical safety was distorted without my knowing it. Because I have always been athletic and strong, and because I have worked with survivors of rape and incest, I viewed myself as knowledgeable, and physically capable of taking care of myself. I would have told you I am cautious and alert but not fearful. That self-description changed many years ago when I had a car phone installed –long before our current high tech world!

On the first day, as I used my new phone, I regarded it as a useful time management tool. At the end of the day, as usual, I left my office and headed for my car. I walked through a dark parking lot, checked the back seat, got in my car, locked my doors, and started the engine. As the motor turned over, the phone beeped and a bright light flashed on. At that instant, I experienced an actual "flood" of relief and safety! At that moment, I realized that I had actually been afraid, and that I didn't know it ! I had learned to accept a certain level of fear as normal! When I experienced a new level of safety for the first time – I could now call for help from my car phone – I understand the full extent of my fear.

HOPEFULLY, NO DELUSIONS

Not perceiving the reality of the environment is potentially dangerous. I was "miss-defining" my reality. Seeing that clearly was both unsettling and frightening. I wondered what else I didn't or couldn't perceive with more accuracy; and today I hope I have become a better, more mindful, observer of my environment.

A PHYSICAL REALITY YOU MUST FACE

Lack of safety is a sobering reality for most women. In our progressive society, a woman is abused every 9 to 15 seconds! And one out of every four women will be sexually assaulted in her lifetime. Living in a society that "tolerates" a certain level of violence against women adds to your feeling that it's hard to count on anyone.

A SPIRITUAL DIMENSION?

Many women experience a deep "spiritual loss" and a lack of purpose or meaning. If you have been striving to be perfect and get validation you have been on a tough journey. Whether you are in the corporate world, running your own business, holding down a 9 to 5, rearing a family, or doing a combination, there is usually a point when you question: "What is this all about? Is it worth it? Why don't I feel better after accomplishing so much?" Or, "Is this where I was going?" "What is next for me that has meaning?"

A WISE VOICE FROM WITHIN

These questions usually come from the "wise woman" inside you, a voice that has been faint or perhaps not credible. Finally, you are ready to pay attention or your "wise woman" is expressing herself loudly enough for you to hear.

Her message, perhaps her challenge, is essential as you explore questions of trust. Her voice represents your spiritual self – a part you may have been denying – not listening to quite enough.

WHAT GETS IN YOUR WAY?

Survival, let alone achievement in the "male world" has demanded a great deal of work and sacrifice. The meaning and purpose that is important to you can disappear from the foreground – stress defeats mindfulness!

THAT BALANCE "THING" AGAIN!

When you don't have time to call your friends or spend intimate time with a partner; when packing for vacation seems like too much to handle and you're lost when you have free time, something is dreadfully wrong….. besides saying, "I'm stressed!" You are losing your sense of what's most important in life, and when that happens, you are also in danger of losing your soul.

ONE WOMAN'S DESCRIPTION

> Susan, a client in her 40's felt her world suddenly come crashing down. Celebrating a desired promotion at a company dinner in her honor, she couldn't sit still. "My body was filled with agitation, restlessness," she said. "I don't remember a word they said about me. I almost didn't care."
>
> Following the dinner, she went home, undressed, collapsed on her bed and sobbed for hours. It would stop then start again. She had no idea what was going on and truly frightened by the intensity.
>
> Several weeks before this experience, she had started her therapy session

by saying, "I feel dry, arid. Those are the only words I have."

We talked about everything she was doing – good and bad and she kept saying "I can't get my 'hands around' this." So we stopped talking. I taught her to meditate and we practiced together for a few weeks, focusing on her body, breathing, and allowing feelings, hopeful she could relax into a deeper level of understanding. Once in a while a few tears came but she still felt blocked.

She came in the next morning after her scare – shaky but much more relaxed. Words came easily. "I think I've wanted this to be simple. I know I have wanted it to be something for you to fix instead of me. I thought it was my family, my husband, my job. It's all of those, but it's also my failure to listen to myself.... to hear some kind of emptiness inside me. I'm tempted to call it spiritual! And I don't even go to church. I don't do any of the things I want to do. I deny the creative, loving woman I am in order to keep jumping that next professional hurdle. And that part of me is actually "yelling" to get out. I give her no permission to rely on anyone, not even me for the real emotional needs I have. I haven't told you, but I'm actually afraid that I'll become physically ill if I don't start doing whatever it is I'm suppose to be doing, being the person I'm meant to be. So I'm going to figure it out! I can even see that learning to trust you helps – trusting you – just a little – I see how absent that feeling is in my life."

SEEING CLEARLY, THEN CHANGING

Susan poured her heart out in that session, realizing she had lost all perspective on what was important and had meaning. What she thought she wanted wasn't working. Everything was out of balance. That next big step in her career always came first. Now it was about trusting something deeper inside and asking for help.

It is important to focus on what's happening in your life – to reflect and understand what affects the way you think, feel, and behave – to be as clear and honest with yourself as you can be. The thing that sometimes makes that hard is a lack of perspective.

A SIMPLE EXAMPLE

Remember the last time you were sick, in bed with the flu, running a temperature. You felt lousy, couldn't think clearly, and time passed in a feverish blur. A couple of days dragged by and your health gradually improved.

When you finally felt healthy again, you realized just "how sick" you had been. To really understand health you must experience sickness. To really understand sickness you must experience health. As I learned with my car phone, sometimes you must experience an "opposite state of being" – to gain perspective.

AND CHANGING?

To understand change, you have to make a change. You have to experience the difference between how it was, and how it is now. You may need to experiment with some simple changes so you can compare and contrast how you feel when you initiate change. Do something low risk so you don't create unnecessary anxiety for yourself.

Examine the realities of your day-to-day life.

What do you see/identify as a typical day?

What is clear/a certainty as you look at the way you live day to day? Or what are you sure of?

What confuses you?

What could you do just a little differently?

If there was a time in your past when you did count on someone, trusted the people around you, what that was like for you.

How were you different?

What has caused that to change?

YOUR HISTORY DOES COUNT

Most of you must examine your childhood and previous relationships, if you want to understand the patterns locked inside your head – those thoughts and behaviors that defeat you when you try to get your needs met. When your resistance surfaces, remind yourself that you are not blaming your family, people in past relationships, or yourself. You are reflecting on how those individuals behaved, what you learned from them, and how you were affected by the dynamics of a specific relationship – and especially by the family system. If you are going to change, you need to describe and understand this system. You can heal loneliness, anxiety, fear or shame once you examine and understand your history.

THAT NEGATIVE QUESTION AGAIN – MORE RESISTANCE

The negatives will return – no matter how much work you do on yourself; however, the skill is in learning to recognize and stop them quickly. Use these responses when you're struggling.

"My efforts to trust and count on people have resulted in a lot of pain. I don't have to keep myself isolated and separate. I can heal this hurt. And if I need help I will ask for it."

"I haven't learned how to truly take care of myself. I don't trust myself anymore than I do other people. I want to learn to count on me. Right now I have no idea how to start, but I can find out!"

"I still believe in Sleeping Beauty and Cinderella. If I can let that go, I can have realistic expectations of myself and others. That's very scary, but it's okay to be scared as long as I don't feel paralyzed by the fear. I just have to start."

"There are people who are trustworthy, but I don't know how to recognize them yet! I can learn about my patterns and make better choices."

"I will learn to ask for what I want. It will be hard to give up wanting people to read my mind. A part of me really doesn't want to!"

"It is healthy and realistic to want to be seen and heard and understood. I just need to figure out what keeps me from getting what I want and need and deserve.

"I see that I need time for meditation, reflection, and prayer. I need a connection to myself and a higher power, as well as to the people in my life."

TAKE A RISK – OPEN UP TO SOMEONE

The belief that you can't count on anyone can be deeply ingrained. Feeling no one really understands you can radically reduce your willingness to keep trying. It is too risky to open yourself to another disappointment – another error in judgment.

This thought process can easily be transferred to a therapist. Now the question becomes: Why on earth would I trust this person anymore than someone else?" If you decide to seek professional help, do your homework. There are untrustworthy therapists just as there are untrustworthy people in general.

If you don't need professional help, stay open to people, but change directions. Your experiences with failure can help you get on track once you understand them. Ask friends and colleagues what they do to be self-nurturing. Start making a list for yourself.

I DO NEED SOME CHANGES

Change is hard work directed at you. You may have spent far too much time taking care of others to be able to "shift gears" and focus on yourself. One client said, "It's like driving down the road in fourth gear and suddenly pulling into reverse!" When you make yourself the priority you might feel torn inside, guilty. Many women report physical pain from this conflict between self and others!

DON'T LET ANYTHING STOP YOU!

You may need permission to put yourself first. You need the permission from yourself, but that might take time. Ask a family member or friend to keep reminding you, giving you permission. You are countering very old beliefs, and it may take longer than you imagine. Internal conflict can cause you to stop, to return to the comfort zone of putting others first and ignoring your own needs.

But as you slowly learn to enjoy, even love being good to yourself, the satisfaction that comes will reinforce you and motivate you to keep it up. You will learn that you can count on yourself.

The old messages in your head may still do battle with your new behavior. The healthier you are, the more consciously you choose who you include in your life. You'll more likely pick people you really can count on. And you deserve just that.

CHAPTER NINE

QUESTION NINE: "WHAT IF I'M LIKE MY MOTHER?"

As an independent single woman, my mother, worked as a telephone operator, drove an ambulance, set a speed record driving her car between the two towns where she and my "father-to-be" lived, and had a reputation for the best legs in three counties. When I think about her good qualities, I'm happy to be like her. She was bright, and funny, and involved, and quite beautiful. I got some of her "good stuff" and I am grateful to her.

THERE'S ALSO A NEGATIVE SIDE

But many times, I have mourned our similarities and feared that I have her dark side fully lodged in my being, my very soul. Then I'm afraid of being like her – the angry, shaming woman who withheld affection because of her own disappointments. She didn't know herself, gave herself away, coped ineffectually with an alcoholic husband, and became physically ill as a result of her codependence and emotional isolation. Two different people! Two different responses from me.

WHAT ABOUT YOUR MOTHER?

If you suffered some form of abuse growing up, you may want to be separate, and to reject your mother as a role model. Even the "normal" mother-daughter relationships produce struggles with different points of view, divisive philosophies, and value conflicts, making distance attractive!

THE WIDE RANGE IN MOTHER-DAUGHTER RELATIONSHIPS

Many women have positive and enviable ties with their mothers. They talk intimately, share their joys and sorrows, and enjoy one another as adults. Others fight continually – or as one client puts it, "We drive each other crazy, and somehow we can't stop." Regardless of the quality of the relationship with "mother" most women fear "being like her."

The best of mothers do things you hope you won't do – or at least not be "caught" doing. Just the other day a close friend joined me for lunch after a painful and somewhat maddening visit with her mother, "What if I'm like this when I'm her age? What will keep me from behaving just like her? she said. "I am her daughter after all. Some of this has to be programmed in me!" These are tough thoughts to carry around unexamined. Talking helps and opens the door to understanding other women share the concern.

AN HONEST ANSWER

But is there an answer? "If you are concerned enough to be examining your behavior, and asking the question, 'Will I be like her?' then it's less likely you'll repeat the behaviors you dislike in your mother," I told her.

My friend was not at all soothed by my response. "I am so ambivalent in my feelings toward her!" my friend said. "I could choke her one minute and hug her the next. She really drives me crazy."

DO YOU HAVE THE INFORMATION YOU NEED TO UNDERSTAND YOUR RELATIONSHIP WITH YOUR MOTHER?

What makes us reject or embrace our mothers? Or experience such intense ambivalence about which to do? What happens to us when we deride and reject her, or when we embrace her too fully? The answers depend heavily on your self-examination. What do you know about your mother's life? What do you remember from the early years of your relationship? What is the energy, the quality of the relationship today? How open and direct and connected is the relationship? Or how guarded and distant? And do you want to explore questions directly with her, in therapy, or perhaps just reading and learning more about what's going on.

BUY ANOTHER BOOK!

I sometimes feel overwhelmed by the amount of literature available on the impact of mothers. Historically, many books have been "mother-blaming," but in recent years, we are getting a more balanced view of the mother- daughter relationship – thankfully. You need a balanced perspective because the connections between mothers and daughters are too complex for any one, simple explanation. Regardless, reading helps until you are ready to examine the specifics of your relationship.

CULTURAL MISINFORMATION

Our negative feelings about our similarities to Mom come from our cultural belief system about women in general; from the frequently interrupted but normal need to become separate healthy adults; from heavy "father/male identification;" and from our resulting internal conflicts about being female.

Consider the effect of the fairy tales, the myths, and the Bible stories you heard growing up. The women are either evil, or powerful in a negative and punishing way – eating children, poisoning or enslaving lovely young maidens, – or they are so stupid they can't find their own shoes (glass ones for goodness sakes!) or can't wake up without a man to kiss them! Not a pretty picture.

THE BIBLE STORIES CAN REALLY CONFUSE YOU!

In Sunday school, at age five, I was introduced to the worst possible image of women – the story of Eve. This mysterious creature was not even a whole person; she was created from the rib of Adam! (Hard to figure out when you're a kid). This less than whole female, using her "unfathomable and fearsome power," seduced Adam and talked him into disobeying his God. Eve single-handedly caused all of us to be "cast into eternal sin!" I can only guess at how much this story frightened me and contributed to the early formation of my feelings about myself.

Women carry enormous emotional and spiritual baggage from hearing negative stories such as Eve's. How can you grow up feeling positive about being female without healthy stories and myths celebrating the endless wonders of being a woman? Couple this absence of literature that glorifies the female with the traditional socialization of little girls and women and a powerful negative force stands in your way – internally and externally.

DISTANCING FROM "THE FEMALE"

Why would you want to be a member of a group that gets less – less time, less attention, and fewer opportunities? How hard is it to fully embrace and identify with such negatives?

Think back to when you were a child. Do you remember times when you saw your mother or other significant women in your life fail to speak out or miss important opportunities? Or do you remember being told, "Little girls don't do that." Or "Honey, don't expect too much." Or "If we have enough money for college, it will be for your brother," or "_____." Fill in the female focused limitation you heard growing up.

WATCHING CAREFULLY

Most women watch, accept, and then, over time, learn not to question. They adjust and accommodate to their situations and to the expectations of others. True feelings – your individual thoughts and aspirations – your identity – shifts to the "back burner." Internal conflict and unhappiness develop, and whether conscious or unconscious, can either motivate you to change and lead a powerful life; or it can push you in the direction of rejection – of deciding you don't like women very much – not even yourself.

WHAT YOU SEE MIGHT BE WHAT YOU GET!

Watching any adult woman who was significant to you behave as "less than" can make you want to distance yourself from the relationship. Regardless of how much you loved your mother, or grandmother, or aunt, if their lives looked unhappy or unsuccessful, some part of you wanted to distance yourself – to be different. Still, watching daily, results in internalizing. The external message about who you are becomes internal – a part of what you believe about yourself. You identify with women and at the same time see female limitations. Now there is a "push-pull" conflict – you may want to distance from your own female identity – and perhaps become more identified with men.

As a child, I remember loving being told, "You are your father's daughter." I gravitated toward him and away from my mother. When I was older, I was pleased when someone said, "You think like a man. That's why I like working with you."

EXAMINING MY MESSAGES

Only in my 20's did I begin to understand the conflict I experienced about being a woman. I was successful in a "man's world," but I felt all the conflict and confusion that came from rejecting my mother, distancing from my own "femaleness," and trying hard to fit in. I didn't particularly "like" other women and considered most of them scatterbrained and superficial. Worse, I often said so!

PARENTAL MESSAGES ABOUT BEING FEMALE

Gradually, I saw I was programmed to gravitate towards men. My parents wanted me to have a better life, and without saying so, perhaps without ever consciously knowing it, they validated me for, traditional "male behavior."

Additionally, they directed me away from the traditional female role. When doing certain tasks my mother found distasteful, she would say, "Don't ever learn to do this!" My father repeated, "You don't want to tie yourself down with a husband and children until you are much older. It can ruin your life."

EXAMINING YOUR OWN MESSAGES

Your messages might be different or less clear. If you were fortunate enough to have parents or adults who helped you understand the joys of being a woman, I still doubt you fully escaped the negative messages. They're everywhere – in our schools, our textbooks, in our peer groups, in the media, and in the minds of men and other women. It is essential to understand them, because if you continue to reject the essence of being female, you reject and harm yourself.

DIGGING INTO THE THINGS YOU LEARNED FROM MOM

Take some time and read and reflect on these questions. If your relationship with your mother puzzles you, your answers will put some of the pieces together. If you find these questions difficult or painful, you can always return to them at another time.

-What is the first memory you have about your mother or primary female caretaker? Write as much detail as you can. Is this a positive or negative memory? Is it both?

-What other memories pop into your head? Write as many as you feel comfortable with. How many are positive? How many are negative?

-What did she teach you about being a girl, a woman? Record any specific messages or quotes you remember.

-What is the quality of your relationship with her today? If she is dead, how do you feel about the quality of the relationship at the time of her death?

-If you could make changes in the relationship, what would they be?

-How will you need to alter your behavior to make the changes a reality?

-Are there any similarities in the relationship you have with your mother and those with other people who are important to you?

-Write your mother or primary female caretaker a letter. This is not to send. It's just for you. Tell her what it was like to grow up with her as a mother. Include both the positives and the negatives. Give yourself lots of time for this exercise. Sometimes just thinking about writing the letter will produce many deep feelings.

-List the ways you want to be different from your mother.

-List the things about her you like or appreciate or the ways you want to be like her.

HOW IMPORTANT IS YOUR RELATIONSHIP WITH YOUR MOTHER?

Our personal conflicts with being female are rooted in our attitudes and feelings about our own mothers. You need to understand your relationship and how it may be driving you in directions you don't wish to go. Too much distance or too much intensity is usually the signal of problems. Forcing yourself to have a relationship with a mother who has done harm to you or distancing yourself from a relationship you enjoy is not the point. Paying attention, in the most mindful way you can, to what the relationship is like, and what you want and need, is the goal.

CUTTING THE CORD

Being your own person is a healthy, rational goal. Because the adult woman in your life is the same sex, you are usually not encouraged to see yourself as separate as early as little boys are. But little girls are often encouraged to stay connected, even attached to their moms. On the positive side, this is definitely how you learn so much about relating. It's also how you learn codependence – being too focused on the needs of others and losing the sense of balance between self and relationships.

Many women feel ambivalence toward their mothers because they can't or won't "cut the umbilical cord." They often don't know how. You have to let go in order to have a connection – to yourself as well as to your mother. That's the confusing paradox.

SISSY AND HER MOM

> Sissy announced in group, "I feel ready to start setting boundaries with my mom." I noticed a couple of members exchange doubtful glances because Sissy had been role-playing and practicing for months without being able to actually face her scary and punishing Mother.

> At 40, Sissy was still a little girl in her relationship with her mom. Her mom came in and out of Sissy's house whenever she wished – she had her own key. Sometimes she alarmed, and annoyed, Sissy's husband and kids when they weren't expecting her. She called several times every day, at the office and at home. She demanded visits, made decisions about all holiday gatherings without checking with Sissy. She bought Sissy's clothes, and criticized her if she didn't wear them.

As a result of therapy, Sissy asked her mother to limit her calls, not to walk in with her key, and not to criticize her. "It takes every ounce of my energy to verbally set boundaries," Sissy told us. "Then I just lose my courage and back down! I feel like such a wimp!" On this day in group, she sounded stronger when she said, "I'm ready to draw hard lines with her. I think I can do it."

PREPARED FOR A BIG CHANGE

Her preparation, in group, was finally paying off. She had made two decisions to discuss with us. "I'm going to ask mother to return the key to my house. If she won't give it to me, and I don't think she will, I will tell her I'm having the locks changed!" She looked around at people's disbelief and smiled, "There's more. If she calls more than once a day at either the office or the house, I'm telling her I will hang up on her. I know she'll be furious and yell, but I'm ready."

I was surprised by her decisiveness. The members of her group were as well. Her previous efforts hadn't worked so I encouraged her, saying "I think you're strong enough to handle these decisions as well as the consequences."

The following week Sissy reported the results. "It's been harder than I thought. Mom was furious when I asked for the key. I told her I was changing the locks, and she stormed out. Then she called me almost every hour to yell. I actually hung up. Now she's quit calling or coming over."

SOME MOMS ARE TOUGHER THAN OTHERS

Not only did her mom stop calling or coming over, she hung up on Sissy when she phoned. This behavior continued for a month, and included ignoring Sissy's 41st birthday! At this point, without the support of her therapy group, Sissy would have caved in. Her husband and children were delighted by the changes and supported her whenever she was in pain about the relationship. She had to stand her ground if she really wanted to be an adult with her mother.

As a second month went by and Thanksgiving approached, Sissy shared with us, "I'm very sad and disappointed not to share this holiday with Mom, but I've come too far to give in. I know she's expecting me to back down but I won't do it. I like this freedom."

FINALLY, A SHIFT!

One evening, a week before Thanksgiving, Sissy's mom called. She asked her what she was doing for the holiday and whether she could help Sissy with her plans! Sissy responded lovingly and gratefully. It was the first in a long series of conversations as they hammered out a new way of relating to one another. This was not a "now everything is good story" because Sissy had to continue to set hard boundaries with her mother for many months. Even though mom kept testing the limits, their relationship improved dramatically. Sissy had created enough of a relationship with herself to feel she deserved a separate life. That separateness allowed her to connect with her mother in a fresh new way that eventually was better for both of them.

One more change was important. Sissy asked her mother and all of us in group to start using her real name – Sandra!

WOMEN DO TALK ABOUT THEIR MOTHERS

I have probably heard as much about mothers in therapy sessions as I have about spouses/partners. Here are examples of what women have to say about their fears of being "like mom."

"My mother is miserable, and I'm fearful of doing the same things."

"I look in the mirror and see her. I talk and hear her voice. It's driving me totally crazy."

"I can't have children. Look what she did to me."

"I have a good relationship with Mom, but I still don't want to live the horrible life she's had, and I just know I will."

"Is it possible I actually hate her?"

"She wants too much and I can't tell her no. Doesn't that mean I'm just as bad as she is?"

"I believe every awful thing she said to me. And I'm becoming the same negative woman."

"I feel guilty when I don't go see her, and I feel awful when I do."

"I love her and I hate her. I just don't want to turn out like her. It would be the worst thing possible."

"Everything I do is because of her. I can't get her out of my head or my life. She drives me nuts."

"My mother is really a lovely person. I'm the problem. I'm just crazy."

"For a long time I felt like my own person. Then I had kids. Now I'm just like her – a bad mother."

"I treat my spouse/partner just like she treated Dad, and I can't stop. I'm destroying my relationship."

"You know, sometimes I think I am my mom!"

"It's like she took over my life, she wants to be me, and I can't be myself."

LOOKING AT YOUR OWN ANSWERS

Ask yourself the question again. "What if I'm like my mother?"

-Write everything that pops into your mind.

-Remember to be honest with yourself. Don't edit.

-Reflect on what you feel emotionally and physically. This can be hard, but it's also very important. I've found that my feelings about my mother, whether positive or negative, are easier to handle once I write them down.

-Write everything you are aware of.

A DIFFERENT QUESTION

"What are the specific things my mother does that I am afraid of repeating?" Or use a version that works for you.

Compare your responses to the first question. See if this process is starting to work for you.

-Can you feel differences in your body when you ask the healthy question?

-Are your thoughts significantly different?

-Are your feelings more positive or perhaps more "manageable?"

-Does your mood alter in a positive direction? Even just a little?

Seeing the changes in how you think and feel, even when the change is small, can motivate you to keep trying. Hopefully, you see that you do have the capacity – the power – to be more in charge of your life!

SOME COMFORTING ANSWERS

You definitely need answers when asking questions about your mother produces anxiety. See if any of these fit for you. And start to write your own.

"It is natural that I have behaviors, attitudes and traits in common with my mother. However, we are two different people. If there are similarities I don't like, I am capable of changing."

"I am learning how much my mom influenced me.   I will keep the good and change the parts that cause me trouble.

"I need to heal my relationship with my mother so I can understand her and connect with her, if possible – so that I can be fully connected to myself."

LORRAINE'S STRUGGLE TO CHANGE HER OWN BEHAVIOR

Changing your relationship with your mother, demands that you look at yourself. That's tough when you know, that if your mom would just stop "it," you could get along with her. You're probably absolutely right. But being right won't make any difference!

> Lorraine's story is a tough example of this. She was in therapy with me for several months before deciding to go into residential treatment for alcoholism. A big change! Her entire family – husband, two adult children, an older brother and her mother attended what is called "family week" in many treatment centers. The entire experience was successful. She returned to my office after 30 days and reported enthusiastically, "I feel wonderful. I'm sober for the first time in 10 years and I feel the best I can remember, physically and emotionally. I've changed a lot of things.
>
> I'm grateful, and I'm really proud of myself. But I'm also scared. My mom isn't changing and she needs to. She's still being her old demanding self, and it's not fair to me."
>
> I agreed with Lorraine, "You're right. But unfortunately that has nothing to do with making things better with your mom. You have to alter your behavior."
>
> Lorraine and I continued our individual work, she attended regular AA meetings, and once a month I met with the whole family. Two months after her return from treatment the family assembled in my office looking extremely stressed. Almost everyone was angry with Lorraine and the feelings were surfacing. She had changed so much and was behaving differently with each of them, mainly by taking care of herself and not letting the family control her life.

CHANGE CAN BE HARD

The resistance to her healthy changes was expressed best by her mother, who blurted out: "I liked you better when you were drunk!"

I watched Lorraine flinch from the sting of her mother's words. Lorraine took a deep breath, and finally responded, "Mom, I have to tell you I really hurt when you talk to me like that."

Marie, her mother, looked at me for help, and I suggested, "You need to talk to Lorraine." Here's how the conversation unfolded.

"Lorraine, I didn't mean what I said. But now you never come to see me when I want you to."

"Mom, I came whenever you called because I didn't know how to say no. I started drinking instead of saying no to you or anyone else for that matter. I have to tell you "no" sometimes to take care of myself. I can't afford to let your needs come first."

"Lorrie, I don't want our relationship to change!"

"I understand that, Mom, but it has to. Tell me what you need from me."

WHAT IF BOTH PEOPLE MAKE A CHANGE?

At this point she and her mother negotiated time together on a weekly basis. Both of them had to "give and take" a little. But Lorraine kept her boundaries. Doing so made it easier to set boundaries with everyone else in the family. Lorraine had to renegotiate every relationship. She could finally do that because she'd learned to value what she needed and wanted. Knowing herself made it easier for her to listen to others without getting lost in their demands.

There were many times during the next year when she wanted to drink again, to give in and do what she had always done, respond to everyone's demands and requests – especially Mom's. Sometimes it felt easier to expect them to change than continued self care and healthy boundary setting. But she held her ground. Today she has been sober for six years. She has a better relationship with herself, as well as with everyone else. She's done it by changing her behavior, and by releasing the expectation that others change.

CHANGE IS REALLY POSSIBLE

The task, as always, is to change. Change the way you relate to your mother, regardless of the nature of the relationship. You can change your behavior without actually talking to her. You can make small changes that will make you feel immensely better – about her and about yourself.

AN IMAGE TO SERVE YOU!

Josie's mom, Betty, came to visit her for six weeks. In her therapy sessions, Josie focused on the unending complaints she had about Betty and her unwillingness to change. I gave her a visual image to use so she could alter the way she responded to her mother. We started the process with role play.

On the tennis court, you often lose when the other person is serving balls into your end of the court. Typical tennis behavior, as well as typical conversational behavior, is to hit the ball back, to respond. This means you are playing the game. It also means the person who is serving is in charge. To create change, you alter this standard behavior – you "jar" the expectations of the other person who is anticipating what you always do. When the ball is hit into your end of the court, instead of hitting the ball back, imagine stepping out of the way and letting the ball bounce out of your end of the court. You don't have to respond!

RETURNING THE SERVE MEANS PLAYING THE GAME

When you don't respond to the first ball served, additional balls will come in your direction. You have to be quick on your feet and sharp witted. If you persist in "not returning the serve," eventually the individual will use all of her or his balls. Now you can serve. And when you do, you can hit the ball wherever you wish. You can change the subject! You are in charge!

Josie's conversations with her mother always went in a direction she didn't intend. She felt defeated and angry in a conversation like this:

TYPICAL DIALOGUE THAT GETS YOU NO WHERE

Josie: "I've had a really tough day, I'm exhausted, and I don't want to fix diner and clean up by myself. Will you help me or can we go out?"

(This is clear, direct, and assertive).

Betty: "You've had a tough day every day of my visit. When was the last time you had a physical? Maybe there's something wrong with you. Just throw something in the microwave. I don't care what it is."

Josie: "You're right, I am tired. I've been a little worried myself. Maybe I'll make an appointment for a check up."

The rest of the evening turned out exactly the opposite of what Josie wanted or needed. She became focused on what might be wrong with her, fixed a quick dinner, and cleaned up alone while her mom relaxed. The next morning she realized she was furious; her mom had somehow managed to avoid talking to her about what she wanted. She wanted her mother to stop it, to change!

BUT IT LOOKS LIKE IT'S NOT WORTH THE EFFORT

You might conclude that her mother is selfish and insensitive. More likely she was doing what she learned to do a long time ago. She changed the subject and did not answer the direct question. She got what she wanted and avoided conflict –at least overt conflict.

When the "new ball"-the different subject- came into Josie's end of the court, she automatically hit it right back. She allowed her mom to change the subject. And with the change of subject directed at Josie's behavior and possibly her health, she was so easily distracted that she forgot what she wanted to talk about!

After many role playing sessions, using the tennis court image, she agreed to try to change her behavior.

COURTING CHANGE

When Betty next avoided Josie's requests for help by changing the subject, Josie said: "You're right, Mom. I have been tired a lot. I'll get a check up. But right now I want to discuss dinner. You didn't answer my question so I'll repeat it. Do you want to help me fix dinner and clean up or would you rather go out?"

Betty: "I want to finish my book."

Josie: "Mom, you are not answering my question." She repeats it.

Betty: "Sometimes I don't think you ever pay any attention to me and what I need. I'm trying to read and relax!"

Note: Here is a place where Josie might finally have thrown in the towel. Mom is good at this! Worn out from the effort, Josie could give up and hit the ball back by responding to this attack on her relationship skills. Mom is good at making it sound like Josie doesn't care about her own mother!

Josie: "Mom, I am listening to you. I know you are relaxing and reading. You and I still need to make a joint decision about dinner. Please answer my question."

Betty: "Well, you're going to have to tell me what it was again!" (And it is possible she was so busy avoiding conflict and trying to get what she wanted that she wasn't really listening).

Josie: "Will you help me fix dinner and clean up or shall we go out?"

Betty: "If you will make reservations for half an hour from now, I'll finish my book and then be ready to go out."

IT WORKED!

You can see how important it is to hold your ground. You can also see how hard it is. Josie did two significant things. She repeatedly acknowledged Betty – what she was saying, what she was needing; and she consistently came back to her original question, no matter how hard Betty worked at changing the subject. Josie practiced and she changed. She took care of herself first, and the relationship with her mother improved.

Once you learn to talk to your mother in this straightforward manner, taking care of yourself, and at the same time acknowledging her needs, you can do it with anyone!

REFLECTING AND CHANGING

Relating to my mother in a positive, loving way was one of my biggest challenges. Sometimes I did a great job; other times, even with all my knowledge and experience, I failed miserably. Part of me held on to the belief that she should change, and she should have! Both of us would have been happier if she could have magically given up her fears, her rigidity, and her unwillingness to show or express love.

FACING REALITY

Eventually I realized she was not going to change. I had to change, and the vigilance necessary in my conversations to stay centered, or to hang in there long enough to make satisfying and productive contact was exhausting. Most of the time I wanted to settle for freedom from tension!

USING MISTAKES TO GET BETTER

My mistakes involved avoiding her – either in my thoughts or my behavior, and then attempting to make up for the avoidance. I tried to learn from my past errors, and the negative consequences; but the pattern slipped back into my behavior. The avoidance went so deep that the first outline for this book did not include a chapter on Mothers! That is, indeed, unconscious avoidance.

Even when I started writing about "What If I'm Like My Mother" I had trouble thinking of what to say! I finally freed myself to write by thinking of the good things about her. Her humor was one of her greatest gifts to me. When I allow myself to move through my anger and disappointment, and the losses and pain we both suffered in our relationship, I find there are many gifts and many things I appreciate about my mother.

FINDING THE WAY TO MAKE IT WORK FOR YOU

I have learned to move into and through the negative, and face my thoughts and feelings. It's all hard, and I don't like it, but feeling allows me to connect with myself, with my love for my mother, for my femaleness. It restores me. You and I need access to "all our parts" and Mothers often hold the key to locating and understanding them.

CHAPTER TEN

QUESTION TEN: "WHY DO I DO SUCH TERRIBLE, SELF-DESTRUCTIVE THINGS TO MYSELF?

"I must hate myself." "Maybe I want to be fat!" "I'm really sick or I wouldn't hurt my body like this." "I'm probably losing my mind." "I can't seem to stop doing things I know make me feel worse!"

SO MANY BAD THOUGHTS!

These are negative messages that flash through women's minds when they ask "Why do I do such terrible, self-destructive things?

Because "the self-destructive things" are behaviors or activities that aren't good for you a seemingly logical question is: "What kind of nut drinks too much?" Or...

> ...eats too much?"

> ...fails to exercise and lets her body go to pot?"

> ...keeps smoking?"

> ...works herself to death?"

> ...stays in a dead-end stressful job that is killing her?"

> ...has one bad relationship after another?"

> ...doesn't practice safe sex?"

...allows another person to hurt her physically?"

..._____"(you fill in the last blank)

WELL, THERE MUST BE SOMETHING REALLY WRONG WITH ME!

The belief that you purposefully hurt yourself, or let someone else hurt you, can keep you stuck forever! For most women, the underlying motive in destructive behavior is not intentional harm. Whether you are eating too much when you want to lose 10 to 20 pounds; endangering your life with addictive quantities of alcohol or nicotine; staying in a relationship that is emotionally or physically abusive, the behavior is providing some "form" of comfort. Granted, it's "backwards." Finding a way to ease or relieve pain is normal. We are programmed to look for relief. That effort is less typically a choice for exercise, healthy nutrition, meditation – all ways to alter consciousness and reduce emotional and physical pain. Instead we move towards something familiar and quick-acting, regardless of the long term impact.

Certainly, the behavior, depending on the severity, can harm or even kill you. Changing harmful behavior is harder if you tell yourself that you're a bad person who wants to hurt herself. Identifying yourself as the problem mires you in anxiety and depression.

A STRAIGHT FORWARD LOOK AT BEHAVIORS THAT WORRY YOU

Sometimes it's harder to reflect and analyze than it is to mentally beat up on yourself. You would be unusual if you weren't doing one or two things you would rather not do.

Consider putting these things on paper, where you can take a look at them, with the following questions. Digging into your behavior this directly can be over-whelming. If you feel it's too much, keep reading and return to the questions later. Whatever you choose, watch and listen to yourself as you write or read.

-How frequently do you behave in ways that aren't good for you?

-Where are you when you do it?

-What thoughts are you conscious of before and after the behavior/act?

-What do you feel or think about before you engage in the harmful behavior?

-What do you feel or think about after you engage in the harmful behavior?

-What do you feel or think about hours later or the next day?

-How long have you been engaging in the behavior? Are you struggling with an addiction? Or concerned the behavior might be an addiction? If you answer yes, to this, please talk to someone in a 12 step program. Look in the Appendix for general information for finding resources.

-When and how did you start this behavior? Who inspired the behavior? Think about how that person might have impacted you.

-Describe the way you want to be. List the healthy behaviors you want to incorporate in your life.

-Who are your role models for this healthier you?

-What changes do you need to make to gradually create this healthier you?

MANDY'S BEHAVIOR REALLY DID LOOK "CRAZY"

I had only been doing therapy for a year when I began to work with Mandy, a 23 year old artist. When she came to therapy in hot, humid east coast weather dressed in long pants and long sleeves, I was immediately curious; but she hadn't come for a wardrobe consultation! She was blocked in her painting.

Mandy was drinking, smoking, and consuming gallons of coffee. She was extremely agitated and had trouble concentrating on her work and sleeping at night. Over and over, she implored, "What's wrong with me? Why am I doing this to myself?"

AT FIRST, I DIDN'T HAVE A CLUE!

Being somewhat new at therapy, I was wondering, too! No matter how much we examined her situation, nothing made sense to her except that she was trying to destroy her work; something was terribly wrong with the way her mind worked against her, defeating her goals to paint. Otherwise why would she get drunk, endanger her health with nicotine and caffeine, and ruin her concentration?

As our relationship grew more solid, I forged into what I intuitively felt was forbidden territory. I asked for more details about her family. She declared that off-limits. Wondering where to go next, I returned to my early curiosity about the way she dressed because she continued to keep her body fully covered, in spite of our stifling summer heat.

Taking a deep breath, I said: "My office is terribly stuffy today, aren't you warm, Mandy?" I immediately feared I had pressed too hard. She flushed, clinched her fists and struggled to hold her breath. A few tears ran down her cheeks and for a minute, I thought she would bolt. Instead she angrily pulled up one sleeve and revealed numerous small round burn scars. I was shocked. I gently asked if she would show me her legs. The same. The scars were from self-inflicted cigarette burns. "Now you know I'm crazy," she said, and stormed out of the office. I was afraid she wouldn't return.

All week I agonized over Mandy. I called her apartment several times but got no answer. I talked to my supervisor, asking if I was in over my head. I thought she was possibly seriously mentally ill. But that thought didn't fit with my experience with her. She was talented, lively, and she loved to paint. I really liked her.

FIGURING OUT THE RIGHT RESPONSE

"Why would she hurt herself this way?" clearly wasn't the right question because it wasn't getting me anywhere!

Fortunately she returned the next week, probably because we had established some solid trust. As we talked about her burns, something in me said she wasn't trying to hurt herself – that she was instead trying to feel better. It didn't sound logical, but my intuition, coupled with my knowledge of her, told me it was true. So I said, as gently as I could, "You must be in a great deal of emotional pain to be willing to burn yourself like that." She stared at me, collapsed into tears and sobbed, "It helps, it really helps! I know it sounds crazy, but it makes the pain go away!"

Therapy really began that day. The severity of her pain went far beyond her concern about her art. Her childhood abuse had been so terrible that she looked for anything to stop the emotional pain and fear she felt. Any self-inflicted pain worked, even if only temporarily. As she got older, the pain had to be more intense to create the desired effect. And it made her feel crazier. Over time, as Mandy expressed the trauma of her childhood, she stopped hurting herself and began to heal emotionally.

BUT I'M NOT THAT BAD

This is an extreme example of harmful behavior. How is it possible to see self-inflicted cigarette burns as anything but self-destructive? Even crazy? Mandy was attempting, in a bizarre manner to stop emotional pain. Early in life, she discovered that physical pain masked emotional pain and she could, temporarily, distract herself from the horror of her day-to-day life.

Because her decision about how to do it is so harmful, it is challenging to see the initial motive was to feel better. Her mind searched for anything she had learned to make her feel better. The "program in her computer" said, "physical pain stops emotional pain." So when Mandy was overwhelmed with traumatic feelings, logically, and not from a desire to self-destruct, she created physical pain to relieve emotional distress.

A NEW PROGRAM VS A NEW COMPUTER

Continuing this metaphor, you would not say, "The computer is broken, there is something terribly wrong with it! We'll have to fix it or replace it right away." You would more likely say, "The computer needs a more effective program. This old one isn't working."

AN "EVERY DAY" EXAMPLE

Here's a more common example: You are trying to get in shape. You have been exercising and eating right and feeling good. It's Saturday, and you begin to think about all the problems you'll face at work on Monday. You go to the kitchen, find a package of cookies and eat half of them. Immediately you beat yourself up about your crazy, self-destructive behavior.

I BLEW IT!

"I was doing so well, and look at this. Maybe I don't want to be healthy, maybe I want to be a fat cow who's out of shape. Why do I destroy all my good efforts? I've ruined my success!" This is like saying "There is something wrong with the computer. It's broken! " What if instead you said "The program is all wrong. I need a new, healthier program."

THINKING ABOUT YOUR PROGRAMMING

You were stressed. Sometime, somewhere you programmed yourself with information that said, "When you are stressed, eat." That program in your computer, or the deeply grooved message in your brain, equals eating. The computer – your brain – produces what it was programmed to produce, and you behave habitually.

You came into this world programmed to live and love. Your system keeps scanning for ways to find alive and happy sensations. Wrong turns or harmful choices are from bad information rather than bad people. Your body, mind, and spirit work together to try to feel good. So when intense and complex feelings are not healed or expressed, and instead stuffed down into the trash compactor, your system looks for a way to change the bad feeling to a good one – even a slightly or momentarily better one. The outcome is dependent on what has been programmed, and through repetition, become familiar and comforting. And many of you have learned things that are anything but helpful.

YOUR ANSWER TO THE ORIGINAL QUESTION

Again, ask: "Why do I do such terrible, self-destructive things?

The answers help you learn the extent of your negative thoughts about yourself. Once you know what you've been "saying to yourself" you can confront those thoughts and stop them when they pop up to stop your progress.

-Write everything that comes into your mind.

-Remember to be honest with yourself. No one else will ever see your answers unless you decide to share them. Don't edit.

-Reflect on what you feel emotionally and physically.

-Write everything you are aware of.

WHAT DO OTHER WOMEN SAY?

It is hard to see yourself as worthwhile when you believe you are intentionally hurting yourself. The original question: "Why do I do such terrible, self-destructive things to myself?" is loaded with negative assumptions and conclusions that damage core self esteem – the thoughts surfacing from the question hurt you. Listen to the voices of other women:

"I must want to die, because I am killing myself with alcohol and cigarettes."

"I know I would feel better – my back pain would improve – if I could get this 30 pounds off – so what does this nut case do? I ate candy bars all week."

"I don't know how to stop working. It's hurting me, my family. My life is on hold. I must hate my life."

"Last month I started exercising. I felt better. Now, suddenly, I would rather sleep later. What the hell is wrong with me? Why do I keep defeating myself?"

"I can never get my body to look the way women are supposed to look! So who cares when it can't happen?"

"I've been in so much pain from the break-up of my relationship. And I'm already in another one! I can't stand to be alone even if this woman/man is bad for me!"

"I go to work every day knowing I'm going to feel sick by 5:00. Maybe I want to feel bad!"

"I must secretly want to disappoint or hurt my husband/partner. I do everything he/she hates. Maybe I want to prove I don't deserve him/her and end the relationship."

"What I do to myself doesn't matter anyway. I don't feel like I want to be here anymore."

"My spouse/partner yells at me, says disgusting things, and I put up with it. What's wrong with me? Maybe I get off on hearing horrible things about myself."

"He/she hits me. I can't leave. And I know that means I'm sick."

AGAIN, REFRAME THE QUESTION

Write a version of the question that works for you, or try this one: "What behaviors/actions keep me from being the healthy person I want to be."

Repeat the reflection process and compare your responses. If you still don't notice any changes when you do this, don't be discouraged. Just keep practicing. You're learning to pay attention to the subtleties in how you think and feel, and it may take just a little longer to notice any significant shift.

-Check for physical sensations

-Check for emotional shifts

-See if your mood is even slightly altered

BUT THE NEGATIVE QUESTIONS ARE STILL THERE

Know that negative questions and thoughts will still pop into your head. If you try to push the negative away, it grows in intensity. Listen and acknowledge the thought or question. Then change your basic answer to something like this: "Sometimes I do things that aren't good for me and even end up hurting me or endangering my health. My behavior confuses me because I want to feel good."

This is an honest starting point. Acknowledging behavior you are either worried or scared or confused about helps diffuse the intensity. If you frequently end up feeling the opposite of how you want to feel, your questions and thoughts are heading you in the wrong direction. Eliminate the statement that your behavior is purposely hurtful because of some deeply held self-destructive or self-loathing motive – or because you are crazy or stupid. And until you feel in charge of making changes in your thinking, here are some additional examples of healthy statements to replace your negatives. Remember it even helps to repeat these out loud.

"Things I've done for so long will be hard to change. I've been protecting myself from feelings I haven't been strong enough to face. I want to face them now even though I understand it can be very painful for me. I am already in pain so I want to change!"

"I am beginning to see the pattern in my behavior. When I realize that I am trying to make myself feel better, I can be more forgiving of myself and focus on changing my behavior. I can substitute a behavior that I know really will help me feel good. I have to learn what truly makes me feel good."

"I've done _____ for so long, I realize I am addicted. I can't handle that by myself. I can seek help from a l2 step program or ask for professional advice."

SUBTLE SELF-DEFEATING BEHAVIOR CAN BE HARDER TO UNDERSTAND

My consciousness of self-defeating behavior was raised in graduate school. When facing deadlines – first with major papers at the end of the semester, and later with my dissertation. I would find myself reading a mystery novel instead of working. Or spending valuable time giving myself a manicure and pedicure!

I felt silly and embarrassed that someone would see me when I was doing the unproductive behavior; but I couldn't get myself to shift gears and go back to work until I had finished the relatively useless thing I had started.

The bad thoughts made it worse. "Maybe I don't want to finish my doctorate." "Maybe I'm afraid of failing." "Maybe I'm afraid of being successful." I always made my deadlines; however, the energy I consumed fighting with myself, left me exhausted. Then I had to spend at least two days recovering!

MY NEGATIVE NUTURING PARENT

Fortunately, I was studying psychology! I came across the concept of the "negative nurturing parent." I discovered I had grown up with parents who encouraged self-nurturing but not with healthy suggestions. Their ideas for rewards for good behavior or comfort for stress taught less than healthy behavior. When I did something well, mother suggested going shopping as a reward; when stressed, disappointed, or sad, she offered cookies and candy!

And frequently she said: "Linda, you work too hard. Take a break. Do something lazy. You don't have to work all the time!" It sounds like a perfectly legitimate message. Not so when delivered at a time when responsibility is called for. I found dozens of these messages in my own head. I had become my own negative nurturing parent: "You've had a rough day, eat what you want/drink what you want/do what you want. It will make you feel better."

A DOUBLE MESSAGE

The messages from this "negative nurturer" are confusing. They say, "Take care of yourself, it is a good thing to do." But they also say, "Do it with something that isn't good for you; or at a time that will ultimately get you into difficulty."

Figuring this out was a relief. I realized the things I was doing – reading relaxing novels and polishing my nails – were not bad behaviors. They were efforts to nurture myself in times of stress that didn't work because they caused more stress. I had to learn to nurture myself and get my work done in a more balanced, healthy way. I still struggle with hearing those old messages. The thoughts dug a deep, familiar, comforting groove in my brain; however, I can usually catch them before they head me too far in the wrong direction. You may never totally eliminate the messages, but you can learn to "turn the volume down."

A REMINDER

No matter what problem you are facing, don't minimize it by comparing yourself to other people who have far worse problems. Being concerned about the things I was doing to get in my own way initially felt too silly to discuss. However, the behavior led to outcomes that were destructive to my self-esteem and to my stated goals.

Whatever your issues and concerns are, they are yours and they are real. You need to examine anything you have labeled as self-destructive or self-defeating or damaging to your self-esteem and life direction.

Blaming yourself when things aren't working, or labeling yourself as crazy or bad, is a signal that your thinking has headed you in the wrong direction. When you use negative words to describe yourself, return to asking healthy questions, and see if you can figure out what is going on. Then take action, one small step at a time.

CHAPTER ELEVEN

QUESTION ELEVEN: "WHAT'S WRONG WITH MEN?"

"Absolutely everything!"

"Absolutely nothing!"

"Absolutely neither of the above!"

When a woman asks, "What's wrong with men?" the answers vary dramatically and the feelings are almost always intense. But the real question isn't always about men. Some women are asking, "What's wrong with me because I can't fix him (or them), or get along with him, or forge a better relationship?" The "him" can be your spouse, boyfriend, lover, father, brother, son, friend, employee or boss. You probably have at least one man in your life you see as "your problem."

ABSOLUTELY EVERYTHING!

If your answer is, "Absolutely everything!" your thinking may run like this: "They are just too difficult." "They are impossible." "They are a mess." "They are violent and abusive." "I am crazy for wanting to have anything to do with him, let alone try to make this relationship work."

NOTHING AT ALL!

If your answer is "Nothing at all!" the thoughts still have a self-negating thread: "There is nothing wrong, it's just me. No matter how hard I try I can't understand my father/husband/_____, so I guess I'm just hopeless. I know he's doing the best he can. Besides, I think women should quit giving men such a hard time!"

BACK TO THOSE CONTROVERSIAL DIFFERENCES

Women and men have differences fueled by both environment and genetics. Historically research and literature have emphasized one or the other; and today we know both our brains and our behavior are different – sometimes dramatically! Naming differences is important because they become tough realities in relationships. The differences create endless conflict, ranging from an impasse about what movie the two of you will attend or where to have dinner to disagreements on the hard decisions about living life, working, and raising families.

Failure to acknowledge differences can block you from seeing the many important and blessed similarities. You must be able to see both so you can stop making destructive generalizations about men and about yourself.

I WOULD JUST LIKE TO GET ALONG

Most of you want to get along with men. You want to resolve the differences, smooth over the conflict, and find ways to connect. To that end, you spend large chunks of time trying to figure them out or fix them. When that doesn't work you blame yourself. Sometimes you blame them. Underneath the accusations, self doubt lurks, waiting to get you!

DO WOMEN REALLY HAVE SUCH STRONG FEELINGS ABOUT MEN?

When evaluating the intensity of women's feelings it may be a toss up between men and mothers.

Check to see if you are saying any of these.

"Men can't be trusted! I don't know how I can make it work with my husband."

"If you grew up with a father like mine, you would know what's wrong with men. They're sick. And I'm probably sick because I keep trying to have contact with my dad."

"My husband/boyfriend is perfect. I should feel lucky to have him. I know the problems we have are just me. I expect too much. I'm unrealistic. The things I want in a relationship aren't really possible."

"Men will never change so I've got to figure this out."

"Why is it MY responsibility to understand? Why can't they get their own lives together?"

"The men in my family are too shut down and insensitive to accept my relationship with a woman. I know I'd be better off staying away from them, but their rejection makes me question my sexuality."

"Our marriage is practically bleeding to death because of him and look who's in therapy! He'll never change and for some stupid reason I keep trying."

"My husband wants to come and talk to you. He thinks if he tells you what I'm doing wrong you will understand it better. Since I don't know how to make him happy, maybe it's a good idea."

"They're not enough like me!"

Here's a general comment that has dozens of versions. You fill in the blanks:

"It's all my fault. I have to learn not to talk about _____ when I'm around _____ because he has such negative feelings about it. You would think I'd learn by now. I'm just too _____!!!!!!"

-Write your own version.

EXAMINE YOUR ATTITUDES

Your own attitudes may sometimes feel a little muddled, depending on your current relationships. Start by again asking: "What's wrong with men?"

Take yourself through the process you've been using throughout the book.

After writing your reactions, reframe the question for yourself or try this one:

"What happens in my relationships/interactions with men that's difficult or painful for me?" Then compare your responses.

USE ONE THERAPY GROUP'S QUESTIONS

One of my therapy groups decided to focus on their issues with men. Here are the questions we used.

-What do you think of men in general? List your attitudes and beliefs.

-Think about men you relate to in your day-to-day life. Which men are you struggling with? List their names.

-Rank order your list. Number one represents the man who is the most difficult for you.

-Start with the man who is least challenging and identify the behaviors and attitudes you don't like. Do this with each person on your list, working your way up to the man who's most difficult.

-Review your lists and see what these men have in common. What patterns do you see?

-If your list does not include men from your family of origin, add them now. Again, identify the behaviors and attitudes you don't like. Look for patterns in what you have written in response to the previous questions.

-Reflect on your behavior with each man on the list(s). What do you do in your relationship or interactions that you don't like? List your own behaviors.

-What do you want your relationship with _____ (fill in the name) to be like? Answer this for each man you have identified.

-What can you do or change to head the relationship or interaction in the right direction? Answer this for each man you have identified.

-Is it possible that you need to either have less contact with _____
or get out of the relationship all together? On the other hand, are you too quick to
distance or terminate relationships? Answer this for each man you have identified.

-If you believe you can't make progress on your own, who can help you?

-What kind of support do you need even when you're making progress?

THE THERAPY GROUP IN ACTION

Before starting this detailed self-examination, the women in the group generally got stuck in blaming themselves or the man they were struggling with or both.

Here's a good example of the issues discussed.

SUE ANN'S STUCK PLACE

"I've given up!" Sue Anne told the group, "I don't have what it takes to fix Bill. Besides he's such a total mess he won't change anyway." In one breath she blamed herself and her husband for their difficulties they were having.

"I know what you mean, Sue Ann, I don't believe there's any hope for men at all," Jamie said.

Beth said, "Would you worry about changing if you had as much control as Bill does? He can afford to be a **!!**!"

Conversation stopped. Laughter and momentary quiet reflected the discomfort with negative statements.

Then Jamie said, "I don't like it when we talk negatively about men. I think we sound like the ones who are a total mess."

"Well, that's truthfully how I feel about myself," Sue Ann said. "I call him a mess when I know it's me."

Sue Ann was stuck in blame. Her immediate response to a conflict with any man was to attach blame rather than examine her feelings and thoughts, and problem solve.

At first the group joined in the negativity. They were quick to blame men and then themselves. The interactions masked the more important and painful feelings of every woman in the group.

SUE ANN BEGINS TO WORK AT A DEEPER LEVEL

I asked Sue Ann: "What do you feel when you talk about yourself so negatively? Take a deep breath, try to relax, and see what comes to you."

Her reply was immediate: "I feel sick to my stomach. My chest is tight. I'm sad."

"What do you need?" I asked.

"I need to talk to Bill about this."

 In our experiential groups this statement meant she wanted to role play a conversation with her husband. We did, and she quickly felt the sadness and pain under her blaming remarks. After a few minutes of talking directly to Bill, Sue Ann said to the group, "I need to tell Bill how confused and hurt I am. And I know I need to ask him what he wants from me that he's not getting."

It had been easier for her to be angry and sarcastic than to face her deeper feelings. Her accusations about her husband and herself masked her denial about the tougher problems in their marriage. In this session she took a big step toward problem solving, and eventually saving a marriage in trouble.

In the following weeks, she shared successful conversations with Bill. She reported remaining calm, listening carefully, asking questions rather than defending her positions; and then telling him she wanted to share her own feelings if he was ready to listen. She asked him to go to couples therapy with her; and eventually he agreed!

BUT MY "NEGATIVES" JUST KEEP COMING

Redirect your thinking by coming up with a useful answer to "What's wrong with men?" Begin to notice how frequently the question comes up in your conversations with women friends and colleagues. Answer the question with something like this until you come up with your own words:

"Women and men are frequently in conflict. It's important to understand the nature of the conflict between women and men without blaming anyone. Sometimes it is hard, because men have difficulty sharing how they feel."

"The differences between women and men are sometimes discounted as unimportant. If they were unimportant, I wouldn't experience so much frustration in my relationships. I need to learn more about the differences and the similarities so I can improve my interactions. I may need help with this."

"It is okay that I get upset about my experiences with men. Many of my angry, hurt reactions are legitimate. I need help learning how to handle my feelings rather than negate them. I also need help learning to express my feelings to the men I work with/live with."

"Sometimes I am afraid of men. My response comes from my childhood and from some of the bad relationships I have been in. I can respect my feelings and learn to take care of myself so that I can have relationships with the men I choose."

"I get so angry with men that I become irrational. I need to understand where all those feelings come from. I deserve an opportunity to express them in a safe place."

" I need help resolving conflicts with men at work. When there are problems or disagreements, I back down rather than trying to talk it through because I am so afraid someone will get angry with me. I know I need to learn to stand up for myself in a healthy way."

"I've cut off all contact with my father because I just keep getting hurt. Maybe I can work on this relationship without talking to him directly. Maybe I can learn to set boundaries when I do talk to him again"

"It's not my job to change men. My job is to look at, understand and be honest about my own behavior and feelings. Sounds like a big order, but I can start a step at a time."

"There is nothing wrong with men that I am responsible for or can fix."

"When I acknowledge differences, I must keep in mind that the way men behave has more value in our world. No wonder saying I am different feels risky even if the differences aren't negative. The problems and inequities come from the way our institutions judge and value the differences."

THE CHALLENGES OF DIFFERENCES

Long standing differences and painful conflicts make understanding essential. Most of us feel more comfortable when the other person thinks and feels and behaves more like we do! We might even agree that life would be just fine if the other person would stop doing the things that cause us difficulty! And that is not reality. We have to understand, examine, and find new ways to communicate about those differences if our relationships, our families, and organizations are going to be healthy and safe; and if we are to enjoy the similarities!"

FEMALE AND MALE "ASSIGNMENTS"

Biological differences are real and perhaps influence behavior much more than we yet understand. However, there is a large and important body of information on the things we teach little girls and boys. One of the biggest differences between you and men is the way you are socialized. The ways in which we "instruct" have little to do with biological differences. The basic lesson is about roles and primary role "assignments."

THE FIRST ASSIGNMENT FOR GIRLS

For girls the role assignment is to focus on and, eventually, take the bulk of the responsibility for relationships. Even today, little girls learn that when they grow up, they are expected to marry someone who will work and take care of them while they take care of the family. If you escaped these messages in the family you grew up in, and today, more and more girls do, there is a high probability that you got them from friends, teachers, books, television, movies, and the growing/exploding world of technology.

Most of you have learned what you are intended to do even if you feel in conflict about it or totally reject it. Increasingly smaller numbers, perhaps as low as 10% of people live in this traditional life style; however, the expectation, the "myth" that this is real life sticks with us.

THE FIRST ASSIGNMENT FOR BOYS

For boys, the primary role "assignment," is to take the bulk of the responsibility for tasks and work. Boys are taught, both directly and indirectly, that someday they will grow up, get a job, and "take care" of a female while she takes care of the family, the relationships. As out of date as this may look to today's young women and men, these early messages hold significant power in how relationships unfold and how institutions function.

REINFORCING THE MESSAGE

Toys, games and play in general also facilitate this learning process. The reinforcing behavior of adults nails the behaviors into place. Kids watch adults carefully, and imitate what they see. How important is what they see? Research conducted in the 70's revealed that at the age of two, children identified brief cases as belonging to Daddy and frying pans to Mommy! Children simply reported what they saw Mom and Dad holding on to most of the time. Even though the majority of women work outside the home, society continues to reinforce these worn out, traditional messages.

WOMEN FEEL, MEN THINK!

Since many assume relating takes more feeling, and working more thinking, another artificial and impractical separation occurs. Girls receive more praise for feeling than for thinking; boys receive more praise for thinking than for feeling.

Obviously, girls and boys all think and feel; however, the approval received from adults and later from peers frequently falls into these parallel categories. You may have been a little girl who was "thinking up a storm" but consider how much the behavior was reinforced. It is more typical that you learned to "feel your way through a problem."

Boys on the other hand were more likely to "think about it" rather than "feel about it." The result is a majority of women whose feelings dominate their thinking and a majority of men whose thinking dominates their feelings.

BUT PUT THINKING AND FEELING TOGETHER.....

Everyone needs to work and think; and everyone needs to form relationships and feel. But our model for rearing and instructing children separates the "assignments" based on sex. Such a model does not work in today's world. However, the model has imprinted your belief system and your emotions. Consequently, you may feel bad or believe you are bad when you don't do what was expected of you.

Regardless of education, values, political or spiritual beliefs, somewhere in your head there is a script about traditional roles for yourself and for the men you encounter. Most women and men expect those traditional behaviors from one another, sometimes out of their awareness. These are hopeful indicators in the millennial generation that a genuine shift in traditional behavior is beginning to take root!

EXAMINING THE DIFFERENCES WITH A COUPLE

Janice, an attorney, and Elliott, a psychologist, came to therapy for help with negotiating household responsibilities and meal preparation. Having both been in extensive individual therapy, they believed themselves to be conscious of their own behavior and their expectations of one another, and were disappointed in their inability to solve the difficulty on their own. Their discussions had turned into unexpected fights.

Both of them grew up in traditional 1950's family structures, where Dad went to work and Mom stayed home and took care of the family. Although she did observe her mother preparing food as a part of her contribution to the well being of the family, Janice wasn't asked to cook, never learned to cook, and didn't like to cook.

Elliott's mother was a nurturing woman and a gourmet cook; and he watched her demonstrate loving behavior through the preparation of meals. He learned to cook. He was good at it, and genuinely enjoyed it. Janice joked about them being a good match: "He cooks and I eat!

A SURPRISING CONFLICT

They believed their arrangement had been working well for their five years of marriage, but tense conversations in the kitchen had become repetitive arguments. As the three of us talked they uncovered surprising feelings. Elliott felt a lack of nurturing from Janice because she seldom, if ever, prepared meals for him. Janice sensed his disappointment and felt guilty that she was failing to live up to the definition of a loving, nurturing woman.

DIFFERENCES RESOLVED

Janice and Elliott were surprised old messages and feelings could be so powerful. Their rational minds said their current arrangement – he cooked and she cleaned – was practical. Using a structured couple's dialogue technique, they discussed their deeper emotional responses, and gradually decided on a change. Once a week Janice would cook a meal. Elliott would stay out of the kitchen, not tell her how to do it, compliment the outcome, and eat what she prepared.

They honestly did not believe lessons from childhood about "proper or appropriate" roles connected to household tasks formed the basis for their conflict. They thought they had replaced those old "assignments." They were wrong. They were also willing to lovingly examine what to do to eliminate the conflict in the marriage.

WHAT DID YOU LEARN TO EXPECT FROM MEN?

Your messages about your own behavior and the behaviors you expect from men can be extremely powerful. Unmet expectations create anger, deep resentments, and sometimes shame. It is important to examine what you truly believe and expect from yourself in relationships with men, as well as what you believe and expect men should be doing when they relate to you.

Whether considering simple household tasks or life changing choices and decisions, severe conflicts emerge from old beliefs and expectations. Unexamined ways of thinking and believing lead to inequity in every area of living and relating. Some of the differences have ugly outcomes – discrimination, inequity in opportunities and pay, and emotional, physical and sexual abuse. These problems are real and numerous, and it is essential to recognize them even when you don't encounter them in your own life. Other women do, and you are each impacted by what happens to others.

DIFFERENT WORLD VIEWS

The separation of roles for women and men carries weight far beyond the specific "assignments." What you learn growing up creates, for each sex, a significantly different view of the world. Women often see things through a different lens from most men. You will always discover overlap and those blessed similarities, but in general, your focus on relationships, and men's focus on work and tasks frequently has you moving in opposite territories.

At work, women are likely to focus on relating and feeling, even while being engaged in a task. Similarly, men carry their working focus away from the office into their personal lives. So as they relate to you, family, or friends outside the work environment, the focus is still likely on working and thinking.

IN OUR CULTURE THE MALE VIEW IS DOMINANT

Now add another important dimension. In our society, the traditional male focus on work and thinking, is still valued more than the female focus. But both women and men are measured by the same standards – those of the dominant and traditional male view of the world.

When you examine society's basic assumptions, you find that "worth" is typically defined by how much money you make, how many deals you have initiated, or how many football games you have won. This unbalanced system creates a major crisis in the hearts and households of most people. In a different world, one that gets less homage or press, the concerns of many women and a slowly increasing number of men, have to do with the health and well-being of the self; of marriages, partnerships and families; and of schools, churches, and organizations in general.

THE IMPACT

All of you know women and men who do not fall into these traditional categories of thinking and behaving. You, too, may be different from these descriptions. Still, most people feel the impact of traditional expectations.

Even though women and men confront traditional expectations daily, the current role distinctions for women and men create an imbalance in power. Women in general are far less powerful than men in our culture. That imbalance in power carries a "truckload" of negative consequences for both women and men; but consider this big consequence for women: It causes you to ask yourself the negative questions you've been reading!

IS THERE A BIGGER QUESTION?

So perhaps there is a bigger question underlying "What's wrong with men?" Underlying the question, "What's wrong with me?" What if the healthy part of you, struggling down inside to get her voice, is trying to ask: "What's wrong with this Big Picture ?"

At first, asking this question is like looking at one of those complex and distorted childhood picture puzzles. You were asked to "find and circle the horse, the cow, the bird" located in a maze of other animals, people, buildings and objects. You begin by looking for what is familiar, for what you know and understand, for what works and what doesn't work, trying to organize a picture that makes sense.

But trying to make sense of your life by looking only at what is familiar doesn't work with this more global question. You need a different picture, a new perspective.

IT'S TIME TO QUESTION THE SYSTEM

"What's wrong with this picture?" is a question about the system in general. By asking it you move to looking beyond yourself. Do it at your own pace. If you start too far outside yourself, you may get discouraged and overwhelmed. As you work to make changes in your own life, you are contributing to the well being of those around you. When you like yourself, you behave differently in all your relationships, in all your environments. You increase your ability to see the bigger picture – and to see it with wiser eyes – and to examine changes necessary in your neighborhood, your community, maybe even the world! You really can make a difference if you start with yourself.

CHAPTER TWELVE

QUESTION TWELVE: "ARE YOU READY TO TAKE YOUR POWER BACK?"

This question, finally, is a positive one. It challenges you to stop asking all the negative questions, and to change your life once and for all.

BE POWERFUL! BE IN CHARGE!

To make changes, you need to learn to be in charge of your own world. Taking your power back and being personally powerful is being in charge. It is knowing yourself. It is making the choices and decisions about day-to-day living and about the direction you want your life to take. It is knowing and saying what you think, feel and want. It's about allowing conflict to emerge, and successfully negotiating your way through those differences. It is about your contribution, your giving back…..making a difference in the world around you.

AND STOP GIVING POWER AWAY

Exercising personal power means creating your own environment. Too few women have the personal power they need. They have given it away.

WAIT JUST A MINUTE! I WOULD NEVER DO THAT ON PURPOSE!

A workshop participant once shouted from the back of the room, "I never give anything away. I'm not stupid!" Her point is important.

Women are not stupid! Women do not give power away intentionally. If a potential new boss said you could have no power at work, hopefully you would turn down the job. If a new potential partner indicated that he or she would keep all the power in the relationship, hopefully you would run!

Given the choice, most women want to hold on to their own power. But women learn to give power away unconsciously. The kind of powerlessness that makes you feel stuck, out of control, or just overwhelmed, comes from not paying attention to the impact, the "cost" of simple, everyday acts and interactions where you back away from conflict, agree to do something you don't really want to do, neglect saying what you most need to say, or fail to put yourself first when it's essential.

ANGELICA DESCRIBES GIVING HER POWER AWAY

"When I first got married, I enjoyed doing things for Larry. I did things even when I didn't want to and didn't feel like it. I would tell myself, 'It's no big deal, Angelica. Or 'So what if you don't get to see the movie you want to see, he's your husband.'

She said, "One simple caring thing once in a while was great, but I started a pattern that continued day after day without my awareness. I gradually gave away my right to have preferences, to need things for myself, to make choices, to decide what I wanted. After about five years of being a 'wonderful wife,' I realized, to my horror, I didn't know myself anymore. I realized I had given all my power away!"

WHO'S GOT YOUR POWER?

To take back power, you first must find out who has it. Sometimes that is immediately obvious, and sometimes you have to do some digging.

EIGHT QUESTIONS AND YOU HAVE THE ANSWER!

ONE. Who do you have the most difficulty saying no to?

This is important! People you can't say no to are usually the people you most need to say no to…!   Even one person who is hard to say no to can become a major source of stress, unhappiness, and powerlessness.

Make a list.

TWO. What kinds of requests are the most difficult for you to say no to?

Do you have trouble saying no to salespeople, to authority figures, to requests for money, chairing a volunteer committee, taking on additional responsibilities at work, taking care of other people, to all of the above?

Take some time to think about the question and identify as many examples as you can.

THREE: Who is the most difficult person for you to ask for what you want? It is likely to be more than one person, so make a list.

People on your list are probably the people you most want or need something from. Not being able to ask means you have given these individuals too much power, creating stress and a sense of being out of control – powerless.

FOUR: What is the hardest thing for you to ask for?

Do you hesitate to ask for the things you truly need the most –time, attention, help? Being afraid to ask for things you want and need causes ongoing internal tension and powerlessness. You may have more than one, so make a list.

FIVE: Who is the hardest person for you to deliver negative information or feedback to?

These people have too much power in your life. You need to express your negative feelings and concerns — anger, sadness, disappointment, regret deserve a voice. Remaining silent overloads your trash compactor and creates stress and powerlessness.

SIX: Who is the hardest person for you to receive negative information or feedback from?

For complex reasons, you shut out information you believe would make you feel bad and keep yourself from getting feedback that might be constructive. Again, make a list.

SEVEN: Who is the hardest person for you to give positive information or feedback to?

Surprisingly, many people have difficulty saying nice things. Being positive, loving and affirming may surface feelings you are trying to avoid. Consequently, not expressing them is giving power away. Make a list.

EIGHT: Who is the hardest person for you to hear positive information or feedback from?

This, too, may surprise you. You may assume that anyone would want to hear good things. If you allow compliments to get inside, you will be "moved." You will feel the contents of the trash compactor moving up to the surface. So if you are avoiding your feelings, you may find ways of deflecting compliments. The people you distance from when they are trying to compliment you, again, have too much power.

Make a list.

SO WHO HAS TOO MUCH OF YOUR PERSONAL POWER?

Look back over your answers. Are the names of one or two or more people on several lists? You have given a great deal of your personal power to these individuals, hoping to please them. They are people you want to like you or love you – validate you in some way. So is there something wrong with wanting to be liked, loved, validated? Of course not. The issue is if you pay too high a price for receiving it. If the goal is only validation or credit, take a look at what your are doing – at your motivation.

Make a list of the people who are on more than one list. Take some time to reflect on how you feel about these individuals. Think about how it would feel to ask them for what you want, to say no to them when you need to….to retrieve a little bit of your personal power.

BUT I'M NOT GOING TO GIVE UP WANTING LOVE AND AFFECTION

Again, the problem is not in wanting love or approval. The problem is your intense fear of not getting it, or of being in conflict with the person you want it from.

Taking your power back will make you feel like a new woman. But practice on someone who is safe! Then you can move on to the hard ones.

SAYING NO IN INTIMATE RELATIONSHIPS

About 98% of the female population is programmed to first focus on what other people want. The more important the relationship is, the more pressure women feel to preserve the connection and avoid conflict at all costs. So why not just do what the other person wants? It's no big deal (Or is it?) if your list is anything like this:

First, he/she is a kind, sensitive, loving _____. (fill in the blank)

Second, he/she seldom asks for anything and is so self-sufficient I worry about being needed.

Third, I like doing things for him/her.

Fourth, I sometimes like doing the things he/she asks for.

Fifth, I frequently share his/her perception that "it" needs doing.

You may be able to add to this list. The issue is how many reasons do you have for complying when requests are made? There are always reasons to say yes. There is great reward in giving to others. But selfless giving gets you in trouble.

The part that is left out is:

Do I want to do it?

Would I prefer to say no?

Do I have a conflict?

Am I too stressed right now to help someone else?

Am I doing something I don't want to interrupt?

Does it disrupt my priorities for the day, the week?

Are my values in conflict with the request?

These are important questions that go unanswered when you don't verbalize a necessary no.

WHY WOULD I DISREGARD SUCH QUESTIONS?

Answering these questions hopefully helps you see that sometimes saying no is necessary. If not, how about at least possible! The wise, potentially powerful part of you would be happier, healthier if you try saying no when it's the best response.

Most women comply when a less healthy, less assertive, less powerful part of you gets "hooked." That person wants to be loved and appreciated, and validated for being kind and sensitive – for being a "nice girl." She doesn't want to create conflict. She is afraid of not getting what she needs and wants if she says no.

SO WHO IS DRIVING THE BUS? WHO IS IN CONTROL?

Who is she? Where does she come from? How does she take control of my mouth?

I ask myself these questions whenever I hear myself choke down a necessary no. I've come to understand that she's indeed powerful, but her power is driven by fear. She's intent on surviving. She's stubborn and hard to reason with. She's little, about six.

She emerges when I am overly stressed, physically fatigued, working too hard, slacking in my self-care, or just generally feeling overwhelmed. Under any of these conditions, I regress easily and quickly. I am out of balance, off center, and the competent, powerful part of me "has left."

THE HISTORICAL EXPLANATION

If you feel little, child-like and vulnerable when facing conflict, you are likely experiencing regression. The "child ego state" is activated by the impression that an adult is "out of control."

My personal six-year-old strategy for fixing it is to make other people happy by doing what they want, by eliminating conflict. Growing up, I was terrified when adults weren't able to function, and I stepped forward to make things right by doing what they wanted. My six year old self does exactly the same thing when I appear to struggle with conflict. That's how I get into trouble. I think like a six-year-old instead of an adult.

By paying attention and working hard, I have learned to stop saying yes when I want to say no. I have even learned to "take back" a misspoken yes. I have also learned to distinguish between making a conscious choice to say yes, and saying yes because I am afraid not to.

What hooks you and pulls you off center is different for everyone. Once you figure out some of the reasons for your fear of conflict, you can change, stay centered in the "grown up" powerful you, and say that necessary no out loud.

REHEARSING AND PRACTICING

-For 48 hours keep a list of all the times you want to say NO but don't do it. Don't analyze your reasons, just practice being aware. You may be shocked by the length of your list; however it truly makes no difference how long or short it is, because you are just beginning to focus your attention on one part of your interactions with others.

> Margaret was initially in tears with this exercise. She said," I seldom say no to anyone or anything! And the painful part is I want to say no almost all the time."

> "I'm really shocked to learn this about myself! And it scares me that I feel so resentful of the people around me." Gradually she learned that expressing herself and saying "no" decreased her resentments.

> She noticed, as many professional women do, that she was more confident in her ability to say no at work more than at home. She examined the differences and realized she had more power in her work role. She said, "My personal relationships feel more risky 'cause I don't trust who has more power. Slowly, taking one relationship at a time, she was able to start a process of balancing the power in her personal life by saying no there, too.

"JUST SAY NO"

Ask a friend or family member to help you with an experiment. For 48 hours you will say *no* to anything the other person asks you regardless of what it is. You don't have to follow through with the "No."

For example if you say no to a request to have lunch, you can go anyway.

You're practicing, and your practice partner must understand and agree to the exercise. Your job is to say no and observe how it feels.

> Margaret asked her close friend Annie to help her. They both found themselves laughing when they realized how good it felt to Margaret to say no. The humor was freeing, and reduced the scare of such a major change in behavior.

IT'S A LITTLE HARDER

With the same person try another 48 hours saying No when you want to, and match your behavior with your desires. If you are asked to go to lunch, and don't want to, then say No and don't go! Again pay attention to your feelings during this period of time.

> In this exercise, Margaret risked sharing her insight about her difficulty with Annie.
>
> She said, "I'm aware it is painful for me to say no to you even when I'm just practicing. I want to talk to you about what that does to our friendship."
>
> This seemingly simple statement was extremely difficult for Margaret; however, it led to several good conversations between the two friends, and they felt their relationship strengthen.

DIFFERENT AND MAYBE EVEN HARDER

Choose a safe person and practice saying, "I want..." Fill in the blank with something you want. Try this every day for one week. Don't be surprised if you have trouble thinking of something at first.

Saying "I want" is about increasing the possibility of getting what you want. If the person says no, you are still potentially successful because you're in a position to negotiate. Now you each know what the other wants. Your power is in the statement of "I Want."

In doing this, Margaret initially believed she didn't want anything. She said, "I want" to Annie and couldn't complete the sentence.

I changed the instructions. For the first week she said "I want" to Annie without filling in the blank. Then in week two she was able to ask for things.

As she kept practicing, she reported, "I can see that never saying no and never asking for anything are connected. I've been 'disappearing' in the relationship because I have no boundaries with Annie."

YOU MAY BE IN CONFLICT, BUT YOU'LL BE CLEAR!

Margaret's next assignment was to tell Annie the truth for 24 hours. Instantly she noticed how much she held back.

Giving both negative and positive feedback, you quickly see how much you hold back from others and from yourself. Use your judgment! If you feel brave, ask the person you choose to do the same thing with you. The time period for this exercise is short because it is hard to do! You can try for longer periods of time later.

> Margaret was stunned at the "unnecessary lies" she wanted to tell Annie in an effort to soften what she called the rough edges of the truth. She noticed how she deflected compliments and criticisms; she either changed the subject or simply quit listening. She had learned to be "polite" at all costs.

When you have grown up being a nice girl, or concentrating on being perfect, you may discover that you seldom tell the truth. Being honest can create conflict – or discomfort. Margaret discovered "unnecessary lies" in her relationship with her good friend, Annie. And that it felt easier to tell the "unnecessary lies."

These little white lies appear to keep relationships running smoothly. The deception may go on for years – at least until you realize you are harboring resentments or feeling distant from the person you want to be close to.

If telling the truth is hard, you'll have just as much difficulty hearing it. Margaret did. If you water down your real feelings in conversations with others, you won't want to hear honest criticisms or compliments. You learn to filter out what you don't want to "absorb" – negative or positive.

SO WHAT CAN YOU EXPECT?

Your observations of yourself when you try these exercises are critical. Write down your feelings, thoughts, and physical reactions. Write and see what you learn about yourself.

THE REAL THING

When you feel ready, you can start saying No and I Want and telling the truth to the people you identify as more challenging than a safe friend or a "practice buddy."

> This next step frightened Margaret. Anything that was so hard with someone safe, like Annie, would be impossible with the difficult people on her list.

> Margaret wasn't ready for her difficult people. She asked two other friends to help her practice. After a couple of weeks she proposed they join her and Annie in organizing a small support group of four. They met weekly and each benefited from the group.

> Each made lists of the relationships that needed attention and hard work. They ranked them in order of difficulty. Starting with the easiest person, they worked their way through their lists, building confidence by role playing – over and over when necessary. Gradually, Margaret prepared herself for taking her power back – for real.

DRESS REHEARSAL IS OKAY!

Practice on as many safe people as you need to, and in whatever format helps, before you shift to someone difficult. Changing your interactions with the people you give your power to is essential for your well-being and for the health of all your relationships. When you learn to say no, make requests, and give and receive negative and positive feedback in a manner congruent with who you are, you are setting boundaries. You are making choices and decisions. Your "psychological muscle" grows and your relationships improve. You are taking back your power! And it's perfectly legitimate to take your time.

A DIFFERENT PERSPECTIVE

The next questions help you gain a different perspective. Write the very first responses that pop into your mind. Later you will want to go back and answer in more detail.

-How do you keep yourself from being powerful?

-Can you "color outside the lines?" Think of examples.

-What would happen if you let all your power out?

ADD THE DETAILS

After you "free associate," reflect and examine further. "How do you keep yourself from being powerful?" means what do you do to defuse, limit, and otherwise just "get in the way" of using the power you have?

Maybe you are repeatedly ill; sleep far more than you really need to; let opportunities go by; hold yourself back rather than being more successful than your spouse or partner. Everyone has her own unique way of keeping her power "reined in." Write about yours.

KATHERINE HAD NO IDEA WHAT SHE WAS DOING TO HERSELF

"I'm just lazy," Katherine exclaimed. Fortunately, she was having lunch with friends who confronted her and said, "You are the least lazy person I know! What on earth are you talking about?"

Katherine had to examine what she really meant. Lazy was an adjective she used frequently to describe herself. But she actually worked very hard, sometimes too hard. She told her lunch friends, "I do far too much of what others need and expect of me at the office. I'm drained at the end of the day! At home I collapse. I lay there, worn out, watching junk T.V. rather than doing something for me, and I tell myself 'I'm lazy.'"

As the women talked, Katherine realized she was defusing her power by not focusing on her own priorities. She was also engaging in negative self-talk and successfully masking her real feelings.

MAKE YOUR BEHAVIOR CONSCIOUS

Keeping yourself from being powerful is generally unconscious. The behaviors that defuse you have become habits – like Katherine's habit of referring to herself as lazy.

You may think such habitual behaviors are just a "normal" part of who you are. Pay attention. Make them conscious. Listen to the off-hand remarks you make. There are lots of clues in the way you describe or talk about yourself, as well as in the way you behave. Your awareness is a first step in your change process.

CAN YOU COLOR OUTSIDE THE LINES?

I couldn't until I was in my late 20's! Even today I have to remind myself it's okay to take big risks and make big decisions. I learned when I was very young to stay inside the lines.

Little girls are often taught to recognize and respect limits set by others. The pictures in the coloring books were already drawn. You were taught to fill in the colors; and god forbid if you decided to create a yellow tree or a green sky! You were rewarded for reproducing things "as they are."

STILL DOING IT!

Years ago I was in a workshop where we were asked to represent our experience through drawing a Mandala. (a picture in a large circle). I was given a large sheet of paper with a circle drawn in the middle. When we shared our drawings, I realized that I had kept my artwork inside the circle.

Most of the other women had done the same. The men, however, had drawn all over the page! When I saw one woman who had drawn outside the lines I was excited until I learned she was an artist. I realized, that at the age of 40, I was still capable of being trapped in such an old expectation, even when I had been encouraged to be creative.

HOW DOES THIS IMAGE OF COLORING IN OR OUTSIDE THE LINES RELATE TO YOU?

Think about all the times you have followed rules established by someone else when it was not in your best interest, not your most creative option. Most of you can find countless decisions that were simply the result of "coloring inside the lines" rather than exploring your unique way.

Changing does not mean that rules get thrown out. But you want to examine them, to see if they are relevant. Blindly following rules often creates insurmountable problems. You evaluate to gain perspective, and then make choices and decisions. Even when existing structures are intended to make organizations and systems work, take a hard look.

"Can you color outside the lines?" is a good question to raise with yourself when you feel stuck about next steps and important crossroads—when you have a great idea for how to make a difference for others as well as for yourself but it feels too risky to try.

WHAT WOULD HAPPEN IF YOU LET ALL YOUR POWER OUT?

This question explores your beliefs, thoughts, feelings, and decisions about power. Your answers will give you ideas about what you fear, visualize with pleasure, or expect to happen.

A THERAPY GROUP DISCUSSES IT

Judy: "Well, if this is true free association about power, I have to say what popped into my mind, regardless of how strange it sounds to me…….I would probably bleed to death! That is really what flashed into my head.

Sandi: "I think it's just an extreme way of saying what I feel. I think I'm afraid of being out of control with power. That bad things could happen."

Ruth: "Not me. I would be myself for the very first time. It feels like a great idea to me. I just don't know how to do it. And not knowing keeps me stuck."

Jamie: "Letting myself be as powerful as I can be feels like people would leave me. How did I learn that? I'm pretty certain I am afraid to make more money or accomplish more than my husband."

Cathy: "I'm surprising myself a little by saying this, but I agree with Ruth. I believe I would be able to finally be myself! Know who I am. And I think I have been making a good start at it. I'm not as scared as I was a year ago.

Lindsey: "I've decided that if my partner doesn't want to be with me when I am who I really am – powerful – that I am strong enough to let go of the relationship. That's really different for me. I thought I would be left. Now I know I might choose to end it. I need to relate to someone who wants to know me for real. Just saying it feels powerful and healthy to me. So if I can do this, anybody can."

THE IMPORTANT RESPONSE IS YOURS

You can see that this question creates a wide range of responses. There are no right or wrong answers. You are where you are. And you need to see where that is and understand it in order to decide what changes you want to make. It is always your choice.

WRAP IT UP

Assuming you have been writing as you read, you have learned a great deal about your thoughts, feelings and beliefs. It's time to shift and learn some techniques for changing or altering those you see as negative or somehow interfering with your progress in the direction you are choosing for yourself.

Take some time to review what you have written about from every section of the book. Consider these categories for your reflection.

-Three to five things in my thinking or behaving that are positive:

-Three to five negative thoughts I have discovered:

-Three to five negative beliefs I have identified:

-Patterns (behaviors repeated over and over) I have identified:

-In my personal life, I have discovered:

-In my work/school/volunteer life, I have discovered:

-Three to five most positive things about me :

-Three to five surprising things I have learned:

-Three to five most important things I have learned:

Include any categories unique to you. This material starts you on your own agenda for growth and change.

POWER CONSIDERED, ONCE AGAIN

Taking your power back means you know what you think, feel, want, need, believe, desire and expect. It means you can speak all that with respect for what others think, feel, want, need, believe, desire and expect. It means you develop your own agenda for growth and change and make your own choices and decisions from a place of intellectual, physical, emotional, and spiritual awareness.

YOU WON'T DO IT RIGHT ALL THE TIME

Having personal power means you don't ask yourself negative, unproductive questions – at least not very often. When you do, you reframe them and start over, being gentle with yourself. You are learning, sometimes one day at a time, to be in charge of and create your own environment, and to take good care of yourself because you deserve it!

So ask yourself the question again: "Are you ready to take your power back?" I hope so!

CHAPTER THIRTEEN

QUESTION THIRTEEN: HOW CAN I GET STARTED? YOUR CHECKLISTS FOR POWER, CHANGE AND SELF CARE

Becoming powerful, starting a change process, and taking good care of yourself can easily sound terribly overwhelming, perhaps even "not worth it." So a quick reference checklist can often help.

USE THE CHECKLISTS

Tear out the checklists that follow, make copies, and put them where you will see them and use them. Each list has space for your input. A checklist gives you that visual reminder, a little psychological "hit" to boost you forward.

THE SHORT LIST

1. MEDITATE, or do a RELAXATION exercise 20 minutes a day.

2. EXERCISE regularly and rigorously at least 40 to 50 minutes a minimum of five days a week.

3. Design and stick to a daily healthy EATING PLAN.

4._____

5._____

6._____

7._____

8._____

9._____

10._____

When you have successfully incorporated 1, 2, and 3 into your regular routine, or when you feel ready to add more self care activities, move to the long list.

THE LONG LIST

1. MEDITATE, do a RELAXATION exercise 20 minutes, twice a day.

2. EXERCISE regularly and rigorously at least 40 to 50 minutes a minimum of five days a week.

3. Design and stick to a daily healthy EATING PLAN.

4. WRITE IN A JOURNAL regularly, preferably daily, and first thing in the morning.

5. Use your journal to write in more detail when you encounter a problem or crisis you don't understand. WRITE A LETTER or a "DIALOGUE" for the person you are struggling with.

6. USE AFFIRMATIONS verbally and/or in writing daily.

7. TAKE YOUR emotional, intellectual, physical and spiritual "TEMPERATURE" several times a day. See instructions in the appendix.

8. Develop a SUPPORT SYSTEM. Talk about your problems.

9. Keep a list of your PRIORITIES AND GOALS. Re-examine them on a regular basis.

10. READ as much as you can and attend WORKSHOPS and SEMINARS for your growth.

11. Make your SPIRITUAL DEVELOPMENT a priority. Explore it at your own pace.

12. Attend 12-STEP MEETINGS if you are worried about addictive behavior, live with an addict, or grew up in an addictive household.

13. Give your CREATIVE SIDE an outlet.

14. PLAY

15. Get THERAPY when you need it. Ask for some form of professional help.

16._____

17._____

18._____

19._____

20._____

MORE ABOUT THE LISTS

Here's a more detailed review of these most important points around your self care, your growth and development, and the changes you make to take back your power.

1. MEDITATE, RELAX.
   - Quiet time is key. The exception is if you are playing a tape. You need 20 minutes a day as a minimum.
   - If you have difficulty sitting still, begin with three to five minutes of meditation and work your way up to 20. The ideal is 20 minutes twice a day. Once first thing in the morning and once at the end of the work day. The most simple approach is simply to focus on your breath as you inhale and exhale; or count your breath…..inhale one, exhale two, inhale three, exhale four. And continue. Thoughts will intrude. When they do, simply return to observing or counting your breath.

   If you want specific instructions, go to the Appendix for resources.

2. EXERCISE REGULARLY AND RIGOROUSLY.
   - This calls for an activity that accelerates the heart rate. The best examples are fast walking, running, swimming, and bicycling. To get the full benefit, exercise for at least 40 to 50 minutes, five times a week. Your body needs time to rest, too, so take a day or two off. On those

days stretch, lift weights. Your body needs some varied form of movement daily.
- Remember if you have not exercised for years or if you are over 30, get a check-up from your physician before beginning any kind of exercise program. Go at your own pace, add time and increase speed gradually. Determine your ideal heart rate for your exercise program.

3. DESIGN AND STICK TO A DAILY HEALTHY EATING PLAN.
- In the last few years, standard recommendations for healthy eating, and the proper balance for complex carbohydrates, protein and fat vary dramatically. The range of recommendations emphasize the importance of your individual needs. Talk to your doctor or a nutritionist for the best individual advice.
- Eat three well-balanced meals of reasonable proportion a day that include fresh fruits and vegetables, whole grains, legumes, rice, pasta. If you are not a vegetarian, include fresh fish, chicken, and occasionally eggs and lean red meat. Before you change your eating in any dramatic way, get professional advice from your doctor or a nutritionist.
- If you feel ready for an even more dramatic move to the right track, eliminate caffeine and carbonated drinks, and lower your intake of sugar, salt, and alcohol. Read labels carefully and gradually eliminate processed foods and "chemicals" like artificial sweeteners.

A BRIEF PAUSE

These first three items are tough! But incorporating daily meditation, exercise and healthy eating will produce life-changing, long-term results. These three things reduce stress and promote healing for your entire system.

4. WRITE IN A JOURNAL REGULARLY, PREFERABLY DAILY.
- You have been encouraged to write, write, write throughout this book. Writing in a journal is a pathway to the inner self. The concept is thousands of years old, a way of opening and maintaining communication with the unconscious. Get Started by buying a notebook and finding a time and a place where you can have quiet and privacy.
- "Journaling" can become a part of your daily self-care routine. As you begin, try not to censor or edit. If you write in a stream of

consciousness with no attention to spelling, punctuation, or detail, your thoughts will eventually flow out of you rather than being forced. If your thoughts are "I have nothing to write," simply start there. You might even add, "This feels silly." "I have better things to do with my time." Then see if additional thoughts and feelings come to mind. If you still can't get started, consider drawing something.

- Historically I have used my journal "when the spirit moved me." That's okay, but I discovered after reading *The Artist's Way* by Julia Cameron that a structure of three pages every morning is even more helpful to me. Try that.
- When that flow begins, you may find you are writing things that surprise you: "I had no idea I was feeling ___." or, "If that is what I have been thinking and telling myself, no wonder I have been so depressed!" Writing brings insight because it helps you "clean house."

5. PROBLEM-SOLVE IN YOUR JOURNAL.
   - On days you feel really stuck, use your journal to problem solve or gain some clarity. Imagine you are reeling from an angry encounter with your partner, a friend, someone at work, or perhaps a parent. Write a letter to the person. You will never send it so you can say whatever you want.
   - "Dear _____, having you for a _____ feels _____ right now!" Let the words of anger or pain pour out on the paper. The process doesn't fix the relationship, but it helps you realize and then discharge some of the intensity of your feelings. You may even discover that you have some important things you need to say to the person.
   - You can also construct a dialogue in your journal. You write what you want to say and then let yourself imagine what the other person would say back. Keep the interaction going until you have nothing else to say. Continue the process until you know what you need to say to the person involved. This saves you from saying things you wish you hadn't said!
   -

6. USE AFFIRMATIONS VERBALLY OR IN WRITING DAILY.
   - An affirmation is a statement of positive regard about yourself stated to yourself.
   - The best affirmations are ones constructed in your own words. Stand in front of your bathroom mirror, make eye contact with yourself, and

repeat out loud your own version of "I, (your name), am calm, relaxed and alert, ready to handle the day effectively." You will undoubtedly feel ridiculous at first. But if you keep trying, you will warm to the process. You may even feel a natural smile rather than a nervous giggle. Gradually you will see that you can alter your mood, and over time, your feelings, thoughts and beliefs.

7. TAKE YOUR "TEMPERATURE" SEVERAL TIMES A DAY.
   - It is a process of checking in with yourself for either a few seconds or for five minutes. Consider how many times a day you unconsciously check yourself out in a mirror. Taking your temperature makes the process conscious and asks you to look at yourself as "a whole."
   - Put your thoughts and your work aside, take two or three deep breaths and ask yourself: " How am I doing?" How does my body feel? Am I breathing normally or holding my breath? Am I moving or working or eating too rapidly? What am I feeling? Ask yourself as many questions as you have time for to increase your awareness.
   - Use that awareness to identify what you need. Slow down and rethink what you are doing, and redirect yourself to positive behavior.

8. DEVELOP A SUPPORT SYSTEM.
   - The more stressed you become, the more likely you are to isolate and withdraw from family and friends. These extremes cut down the much-needed opportunity to talk about what is happening in your life.
   - Support systems come in a variety of shapes and sizes. A few good friends may be what you need, as long as you can be honest and open about your true feelings. It could be a group of colleagues, or a mix of friends and people you don't know. The point is to have a place you know you will go regularly to talk.
   - A support group has no therapist; everyone is equal. So rules are important. Talk about confidentiality, expectations, purpose and goals, appropriate ways to give one another feedback vs. advice. You can find many books that give you ground rules for getting a support group started.

9. KEEP A LIST OF YOUR PRIORITIES AND GOALS.
   - Re-examine your list on a regular basis. Yes, more writing! It helps to see what you were thinking six weeks or six months ago. But goals and

priorities are not intended to be encased in cement; they are guidelines, benchmarks, ways of measuring where you have been, where you are, and where you want to go. Use them to see if you are talking care of yourself and doing the things you believe are most important to you.

- You don't need a particular format. Just try writing the five to ten (or more) things you want to accomplish in your life. Then rank order them. Write as much about each goal as you can. If your top five things turn out to be getting very little of your time and attention, examine whether your goals and priorities have changed or whether your self-care is slipping.

10. READ AS MUCH AS YOU CAN AND ATTEND WORKSHOPS AND SEMINARS FOR YOUR GROWTH AND DEVELOPMENT PERSONALLY AND PROFESSIONALLY.

- Think about what you believe you need and want to learn. What skills do you hope to develop?
- You can create your own learning program. Gather some friends and colleagues who want to learn more about becoming assertive or how to negotiate or manage conflict; buy a book on the subject; and get together regularly to read, share your ideas, and practice on each other with role-plays.
- When Dr. Harriet Lerner's first book, <u>The Dance of Anger</u>, came out, many women's groups formed to learn more about expressing anger appropriately. Many groups have been formed using my book *Release from Powerlessness: Take Charge of Your Life* Whatever you are hoping to learn, someone else is too; and there is a book to help! New ideas keep you growing and changing, and that's a big part of what you need to stay healthy, happy and powerful.

11. MAKE YOUR SPIRITUAL DEVELEMENT A PRIORITY.

- Remember that spirituality and religion are different. If you feel stuck, the *The Spirituality of Imperfection* by Ernest Kurtz and Katherine Ketcham is a great place to begin your exploration. If you are in search of a spiritual community, or more information on how to get started, consider talking to someone in the faith you grew up in or step outside that tradition and talk to a Unity, Unitarian, or Buddhist minister.

12. ATTEND 12-STEP MEETINGS IF YOU ARE WORRIED ABOUT ADDICTIVE BEHAVIOR, LIVE WITH AN ADDICT, OR GREW UP IN AN ADDICTIVE HOUSEHOLD.

- If you are unfamiliar with these programs, contact First Call (formally The National Council on Alcoholism and Drug Dependence) in your community. That office can give you locations of meetings for any of the addiction or addiction related problems you are struggling with. Anyone can attend a meeting; however, you need to determine what meetings are "open" and which ones are "closed."
- Closed meetings are for individuals who have acknowledged they are addicted. Open meetings are for addicts and their family members, friends, and colleagues who want to learn about AA, or for those who are truly uncertain of the extent of their problems and need a safe place to go for information.
- 12-Step programs can be a great source of support and strength for you. Try as many different groups as you need to find one that feels right for you.
- Also be aware there are options to traditional 12-steps. The 13 steps, for example, is a more recent approach to working with addictions.

13. GIVE YOUR CREATIVE SIDE AN OUTLET.

- Exploring your creativity doesn't mean you will become a great painter or pianist; but it does mean you could develop a beautiful garden, learn to cook great ethnic dinners, enjoy photography, sing in a choir, write poetry, or draw stick figures! Everyone needs to attend to this part of the self.

14. PLAY.

Release the "kid energy" inside you. Your "child ego state" encompasses your feelings, your creativity, your spontaneity, your playfulness. Play and creative activities help you develop this essential part of who you are.

- Playing can become one of the best things you do for yourself. It can also be the hardest. Think back to childhood. What did you love to do? What did you always want to do? Consider flying a kite, blowing bubbles, playing baseball, running in the rain, inventing games, watching funny movies, doing anything you can think of that sounds fun, and relaxing.

15. GET THERAPY WHEN YOU NEED IT.

- Asking for help is a sign of strength, wisdom, and mental health. If you try these suggestions and you still feel flat or depressed, seek professional help. Please don't try to do it alone when you know you are not getting better. You deserve the help, whatever it may be.

IT REALLY IS OVERWHELMING!

Deciding to make your life better – healthier and happier and more focused – obviously takes hard work. As you tackle one difficult thing at a time, you develop more of that psychological muscle. You feel better emotionally, and become more confident. You have a growing sense that you deserve to feel better, and to have your life go in the direction you desire.

But the hard work is the reality. You will always have problems and hardships and painful choices, even if you read dozens of books and go to therapy. A big part of taking care of yourself, taking charge of your life and being truly powerful is facing that reality. Accepting your own unique life, with all its "warts" as well as its beauty, allows you to cherish it for what it is.

AND FINALLY

Remember that taking charge of your life, becoming a powerful person, does not mean that you always get your way or that you have only happen endings in your future. Nor does it mean that you stop having painful or angry feelings. It does mean that you are conscious and you know what is going on in your own head, in your own heart. You can see yourself, and when it's safe and appropriate, you can let others see you.

Additionally, you have tools and techniques to help you with whatever problem you are suddenly facing. You know how to deal with the pain and the disappointment you legitimately feel when things go wrong.

To make these changes easier demands a kind of "surrender," a letting go, or what some would call a leap of faith. The surrender is to your own higher self; the letting go is giving up a belief in control; and the leap of faith is with yourself and the relationship or situation you want to improve.

You can make the changes you want to make in your life. Most importantly, you can learn to ask yourself the right questions, and make the choices that are best for you and for the people you love. Whenever it gets hard, remember a quote from Eleanor Roosevelt. "You must do the thing you think you cannot do."

When you believe in your ability to take just one step forward, you will feel your own progress and sense your ability to keep moving. Do it for yourself and everyone you know and love will benefit!

APPENDIX A.

MORE IDEAS FOR SELF CARE AND SELF EXAMINATION

BEGINNING JOURNAL IDEAS

If you decide to start writing in a journal and don't know how to start, try this. Commit to writing just four basic sentences each day by answering these questions.

-If you close your eyes and reflect, what is going on with your body? Relaxed/tense? Tired/energetic? Identify anything you are aware of in any part of your body.

-What are you thinking about? List any thoughts that you are aware of in the foreground of your mind.

-What are you feeling? Happy; sad; angry; lonely; loving; confused?

-What, if any, spiritual awareness do you have? A connection to a power greater than you? A connection to nature, the universe?

You will find that reflection on these questions will slowly expand from one sentence to several, and then you can write as little or as much as you want. Regardless, you are practicing self awareness, and it will help you each day.

RELAXATION TECHNIQUES

-Relaxed Breathing. Sit quietly, close your eyes, and breathe using the following "formula" – Breathe in to the count of 4; hold your breath to the count of 7; exhale, slowly, to the count of 8. Repeat this 4 times. You can repeat it another 4 times. You will need to practice to find your own pace. Breathe normally. You can use this as many times a day as you find useful. Consider practicing before and/or after a difficult meeting or conversation.

-Taking Your Temperature. Referring back to the questions for journal writing, you can check in with yourself – Take Your Temperature – any time during the day. It centers you to just sit and ask what am I feeling in my body? What am I thinking? What am I feeling? Do I feel connected to any sense of that which is greater than self? This is simply a way to focus, calm, and re-direct your energy and actions.

-Basic Meditation Technique. Meditating daily will improve your emotional and physical well-being. In the resources/bibliography you will find references for meditation, but here is a basic technique. Sit with your eyes closed. Spine straight and feel flat on the floor. Take a few deep, clearing breaths and then begin to focus on your breath and count. Inhale to the count of 4, pause for a count of 2, exhale to the count of 4, pause to the count of 2 and repeat. Try doing this for approximately 20 or 30 minutes. If that feels too difficult, start with 5 or 10 and build up gradually.

SELF-SYSTEM ANALYSIS

1. SELF

    Take a long hard look at who you are today—personally and professionally. What do you value most?

    What are your strengths and weaknesses?

    What are your goals and priorities?

    How do you feel about yourself?

    What do you like most about yourself?

    What do you dislike most about yourself?

    What needs to be changed?

2. ATTITUDES AND BELIEFS

    What do you believe about being a woman?

    What are your assumptions about life?

    What are your expectations for your life?

Do you feel like a victim or do you believe you are in charge of your life?

3. BEHAVIOR

Is your behavior congruent with your values, goals, priorities, attitudes, and beliefs?

Do you find that you say one thing and do another? If so, do you understand this behavior?

Do you seek contacts and work opportunities with and for other women?

4. FEEDBACK

How do others perceive you?

Is the feedback you receive positive, negative, inconsistent, or is there an absence of feedback?

Do you know people whom you trust to ask for information on how you are regarded, both personally and professionally?

Are you willing to ask for such data, listen to it, evaluate it, use it?

5. SITUATION

What are the specific situations in your life that you find problematic?

Who are the people involved?

What is the nature of the interaction, the work to be done?

When does the conflict or difficulty emerge?

What resources do you have for confronting the problems?

6. ENVIRONMENT

What is your immediate environment like? What is your family life like?

Describe your work or volunteer life?

How would you describe the "climate"? Or if you were taking the temperature, what would it be?

Do you find that you feel your home or work settings are a crazy place to be?

Who are the people that make your home or work place seem crazy?

What kind of work do you do?

How do you or your superiors organize your work?

What is the day like?

How does the day flow?

Do you feel valued as a person and as a professional?

7.   SYSTEMS (Think of a system that you function in today.)

How well do you understand the entire system?

Where are the sources of formal and informal power?

Who is in charge?

What are the system's values?

What is the system's true attitude toward women?

What resources do you have access to within the system?

Are you using an existing network within the system?

Could you start a networking group?

DECADES ANALYSIS

To understand your history...what you were taught about life... and particularly what you were taught about power... reflect on the decades of your life.

In each 10 year period, think about, then write anything relating to what you might have learned about power...positive or negative.

1 to 10

10-20

20-30

30-40

40-50

50-60

60-70

70-80

When you have completed the decade bringing you to the present, go back and see if you can "name" each decade.

(For example, one woman named the first ten years of her life "negative overempowerment." She was taught that she could do anything she wanted. A great message if she had also been told about normal limitations and what to do when facing them. Not getting that second part caused her great pain and frustration when she bumped into challenges difficult to handle.)

STRESS ANALYSIS IN BRIEF

-Where are you when you feel stressed?

-Who are you with?

-Who does this person remind you of?

-When have you felt this way before?

-What are you physical symptoms? Emotional symptoms? Thoughts?

-Are you having any symptoms that frighten or concern you? If so, who could you talk to?

-Do you know of anything you could do that would help you feel better? And does something healthy come to mind – like getting some exercise, meditating, talking to a friend, resting – vs old negative coping techniques – like too much food or alcohol?

-Can you construct a plan for reducing your stress or do you need to ask for help?

USING AFFIRMATIONS

Remember an affirmation is a positive statement made to self ABOUT self. An all purpose example: I _____ insert your name, like and love myself unconditionally.

State and/or write the statement and then wait for the disclaimer that will pop into your mind. There may be MANY disclaimers that come to you. Write them down. Slowly learn to challenge them. What is the truth? Learn, again as you have throughout the book, to examine the exaggerations and distortions and reframe the statement into the truth.

For a reference and many examples, look for I Deserve Love by Sandra Ray. It has been out of print for some time, but perhaps you can search on line.

WHAT IS AN INTENSIVE?

I reference "an intensive" in one or two of my client case examples. When I owned a clinic called Centerpoint, we did these week long experiential groups. They allowed exploring personal problems in great depth. You can find similar groups offered in the following locations:

COTTONWOOD TREATMENT CENTER in Tucson AZ

THE MEADOWS TREATMENT CENTER in Wickenberg, AZ

THE CARON TREATMENT CENTERS in New England

12 STEP PROGRAMS

Today all you need to do is get on line and look for 12 step programs in your city. Typically you can find an AA meeting or an NA meeting or Alanon or Codependence meeting almost every night – or at least weekly.

If you are not drawn to 12 step programs, search for the 13 steps. This is a program that has a practical vs. a spiritual approach.

APPENDIX B

A BIBLIOGRAPHY OF FAVORITE BOOKS – WITH GRATITUDE!

Numerous amazing authors, thinkers, and colleagues and friends have influenced my thinking and writing, and I am genuinely grateful. This list is made up of those I count as favorites – the ones whose ideas "infiltrated" my mind. Read them when and as you can or are inclined to – and grow from the thinking of these writers as I believe I have.

Beyond Sex Roles – Alice Sargent – An early and amazing book. Alice was a dear friend

Women's Realities – Anne Wilson Schaef – A month long intensive with Anne helped me embrace my challenges and put me on track

The Dance of Anger; The Dance of Deception; The Dance of Intimacy – Harriet Lerner – An amazing thinker and writer

What do Women Want; Understanding Women – Luise Eichenbaurmand Susie Orbach – Their theory supported what I was writing and speaking about and built my confidence

The Addicted Organization – Diane Fassell & Anne Wilson Schaef…Diane is a good friend and a systems thinker

The Assertive Woman – Phelps and Austin –Ground breaking ideas I have used since the 70's

The Tao of Leadership – John Heider – a special friend and a great therapist for me in my work on myself

In the Absence of the Sacred – Jerry Mander – just a different "take"

Seeing Systems – Barry Oshry – A great mind – He shaped my thinking in the early 70's

Let Your Life Speak – Parker Palmer – Just a good and thoughtful book for your reflections

A Gift from the Sea – Anne Morrow Lindberg – A book I always take on ocean vacations – stands the test of time and thinking

The Empowered Manager and *The Answer to How is Yes* – Peter Block – brilliant thinker – an "out of the box" approach

The Transformers – Jackie Small – Learned holotropic breath work from her. Good writer!

In a Different Voice – Carol Gilligan – ground breaking research and writing for understanding girls and women

Buddha's Brain – The Practical Neuroscience of Happiness and Love and Wisdom

Just One Thing – Rick Hanson – pushing me into new ways of thinking – genuine, caring person.

The Happiness Hypothesis – Jonathan Haidt – filled with research on who we are, how we think.

I am influenced in the foundational concepts of this book by Dr. Albert Ellis and Dr. David Burns …

See *A Guide to Ration Living* by Elis

And Feeling Good – the New Mood Therapy by Burns

In Burns you'll find a list of the 10 basic thought distortions of most *of us*.

APPENDIX C

BIBLIOGRAPHY/RECOMMENDED READING

The Lens of Gender – Sandra Bem

All That is Solid Melts Into Air – Marshall Berman

Where to Go From Here – James E. Birren and Linda Feldman

On Dialogue – David Bohm

Stewardship – Peter Block

Women's Inhumanity to Women – Phyllis Chessler

The Tao of Negotiation – Joel Edelman and Mary Beth Crain

Circle of Stones: Woman's Journey to Herself – Judith Duerk

The Power of Partnership – Riane Eisler

The First Sex – Helen Fisher

The Tipping Point – Malcolm Galdwell

The Birth of Pleasure – Carol Gilligan

Real Power – Janet Hagberg

Buddha's Brain: The Practical Neuroscience of Happiness, Love, and Wisdom – Rick Hanson &
 Richard Mendius

Dialogue and the Art of Thinking Together – William Isaacs

Leadership: The Inner Side of Greatness – Peter Koestenbaum

Facing the World With Soul – Robert Sardello

The Confident Woman – Marjorie Schaevitz

How Can I Get Through to You – Terrance Real

Why So Slow – Virginia Valian

Addiction to Perfection – Marion Woodman

Crucial Conventions – Kerry Patterson, Joseph Grenny, Ron McMillan and Al Switzler

Arbinger Institute. *Leadership and Self-Deception: Getting out of the Box,* San Francisco, CA 2010

Belinkey, Mary Field; Clinchy, Blythe McVicker; Goldberger, Nancy Rule; Torule, Jill Mattuch. *Women's Ways of Knowing.* Basic Books, N.Y., 1986.

Gendlin, Eugene. *Focusing.* New York, Bantam Books, 1981.

Goulding, Mary and Goulding, Robert. *Changing Lives Through Redecision Therapy.* Brunner/Mazel Publisher, New York, 1979.

Hanson, Rick and Mendius, Richard. *Buddha's Brain: The Practical Neuroscience of Happiness, Love, and Wisdom, 2009*

Josefowitz, Natasha. *Paths to Power.* Addison-Wesley, Reading MA., 1980.

Lerner, Harriet. *The Dance of Anger.* Harper and Row, New York, 1985.

Missildine, Hugh. *Your Inner Child of the Past.* New York, Pocket Books, 1963.

Patterson, Kerry; Grenny, Joseph; McMillan, Ron and Switzler, Al. *Crucial Conversations – Tools for Talking When Stakes are High.*

Pollard, John K. *Self-Parenting.* Generic Human Studies Publishing, Malibu, CA., 1987.

Ray, Sondra. *I Deserve Love.* Les Femmes, Millbrae, CA., 1976.

Schaef, Anne Wilson. *Women's Realities – An Emerging Female System in the White Male Society.* Winston Press, Inc., Minneapolis, 1981.

Sargent, Alice. *The Androgynous Manager.* AMACOM, a division of American Management Associations, New York, 1981.

Shaevitz, Marjorie. *The Superwoman Syndrome.* Warner Books, New York, 1984.

Subby, Robert and Fried, John. *Co-dependency and Family Rules.* Health Communications, Inc., Pompano Beach, Florida, 1984.

Warschau, Tesa Albert. *Winning by Negotiation.* Berkley Books, New York, 1981.

Welsh, Mary Scott. *Networking.* Harcourt, Brace, Jannovich, New York, 1980.

Whitfield, Charles. *Healing the Child Within.* Health Communications, Inc., Pompano Beach, Florida, 1987.

CONTACT INFORMATION

MY WEBSITE AND BLOG…

I invite you to visit my website and read my blog whenever you are interested. I write regularly on psychological, feminist, and political issues. I welcome questions and challenges, as well!

www.drlindalmoore.com

DEFINITIONS OF POWER

If power still feels a bit illusive to you, I invite you to read my first book, *Release from Powerlessness: Take Charge of Your Life.* You can order it on Amazon or from my website.

You'll also find other references on power in the bibliography and recommended readings.

ABOUT THE AUTHOR

Dr. Linda L. Moore is a licensed psychologist practicing in Kansas City, Missouri. She is President of Linda L. Moore and Associates, a company which offers individual and group therapy, executive coaching, management consulting and presentations for organizations and associations around the country. Additionally, she is the former President and Co-Founder of CenterPoint, an outpatient counseling center. Dr. Moore has worked extensively throughout the United States and abroad and is known for her work as hostess of a radio talk show, a contributing editor for Kansas City's ABC TV affiliate, and her work with women, addictions, management, leadership training, stress and human relationships.